PAUL GAYLER'S

SAUCE book

PAUL GAYLER'S

SAUCE book

300 world sauces made simple

Photography by Richard Jung

Kyle Cathie Limited

First published in Great Britain in 2008 by
Kyle Cathie Limited
www.kylecathie.com

ISBN hardback 978-1-85626-897-4

Edited by Caroline Taggart
Designed by Jane Humphrey
Home economy by Linda Tubby
Styling by Roisin Nield
Copy editor Sally Somers
Proofreader Ruth Baldwin
Index by Sarah Ereira
Production director Sha Huxtable

Paul Gayler is hereby identified as the author of this work in accordance with Section 77 of the Copyright, Designs and Patents Act 1988.

A Cataloguing in Publication record for this title is available from the British Library.

Printed in China by
C&C Offset Printing Co.

Acknowledgements

I gratefully acknowledge the tremendous support of the following people, without whom this book would not have been possible:

Good friends Linda Tubby and Richard Jung, food stylist and photographer, who between them brought the sauces and recipes to life.

Roisin Nield, for her wonderful prop styling, as usual.

Jane Humphrey, for the gorgeous design.

Copy editor Sally Somers, for her support and putting the book together beautifully.

Jane Middleton, respected friend, for her help and advice.

Lara Mand, as ever, for a great job on the initial typing of the text.

My chefs, whose help on a daily basis and dedication to fine food help to make writing a book possible.

A special thanks to Caroline Taggart – I deeply value her support, friendship and professionalism in helping me create a lovely book.

DEDICATION

To my family, for their constant support for my writing, and their encouragement.

contents

INTRODUCTION

A good sauce can make a meal. Think of a rich, creamy cheese béchamel poured over tender cauliflower florets, a sweet, aromatic tomato and basil sauce tossed with fresh pasta, or a light, vanilla-scented custard drizzled round a slice of apple pie – simple marriages made in heaven.

Sauce is a French word, originally taken from the Latin *salsus*, meaning salted. Classically, a sauce is a flavourful liquid that has been thickened in one of several standard ways and used to accompany or coat a food. Nowadays, the definition has expanded to include not just classic French-style sauces but salsas, relishes, chutneys and dressings too. All these add flavour, colour, texture and moisture to food, and can even make it easier to digest.

For many, the idea of making at home the kind of sauces we enjoy in restaurants can be downright scary. But it's a lot easier than you might think, and doesn't have to be time-consuming or complex. Once you understand the various sauce 'families' and have mastered a few basic techniques, it will open up the way to making a multitude of different sauces, and even creating your own versions. The key to success with sauces is to ensure that they complement and enhance the food they are to be served with. They should never overpower a dish, but should have a clean, well-defined flavour and a pleasing texture and consistency.

Although sauces are strongly associated with French cooking, they are an essential element in every cuisine. Now that global travel is available to all, we are more curious about the food of other cultures; at the same time our supermarkets stock a massive range of ingredients from all over the world. As a result, the scope for experimenting with sauces has increased enormously.

It's a shame that so many home cooks reach for a bought sauce rather than making their own. Commercial sauces are often laden with thickeners, colourings, preservatives and other additives. They tend to have an unappetising, gloopy consistency and frequently lack any flavour at all. Making fresh sauces at home will enhance your cooking beyond recognition. And although some require a degree of skill and judgement, others can be as simple as whizzing a few ingredients in a blender to make a pesto or relish, or briefly cooking berries with a little sugar to strain and serve as a fruit coulis.

When I set out to write this book, I wanted to show that creating great sauces was within the reach of any home cook. Many sauces can easily be put together in the time it takes for the rest of the meal to cook, and a surprising number of them require no cooking at all. Some, especially the French classics, take rather longer and may require a good stock base. If you don't have the time or the inclination to make your own stock, simply buy the best ready-made stock you can (the fresh ones in cartons are usually good, but check the ingredients: they should all be ones you would use at home).

The book is divided into five geographical regions: France (covering the 'classic' French sauces), Europe and the Mediterranean, the Americas, Asia, and the Pacific Rim. There is also a chapter on fusion food, called East Meets West, and one on sweet sauces. These divisions are not intended to be rigid, and there is plenty of overlap between the regions, so please don't feel constrained by them.

Sauces make a fantastic shortcut to different cultures and cuisines. You can give a piece of plain grilled fish or meat a French, Italian, Indian or Mexican character, depending on whether you serve it with hollandaise, salmoriglio, raita or chimichurri. You can flavour a basic sauce with hot chillies for an Asian or South American accent, with cheese, horseradish or anchovies for a European feel, or with herbs and aromatics such as lemon and garlic for a taste of the Mediterranean. And when it comes to desserts, you can be utterly indulgent: who can resist butterscotch sauce or a dark, rich hot chocolate sauce drizzled over ice cream?

A BRIEF HISTORY OF SAUCE-MAKING

In the days before refrigeration, sauces were often used to mask foods that were thought to be tainted in flavour. The Romans were the first to disguise dubious freshness in this way; they also used saucing as an opportunity to demonstrate the variety of costly spices the host had available. This practice continued well into the Middle Ages. Looking through old recipes in my own collection of cookery books, I notice that sauces were often so heavily spiced and seasoned that it must have been almost impossible to single out any particular flavour, never mind taste the food underneath.

It was the French who developed the kind of sauces we are familiar with in the West today. At the beginning of the nineteenth century, Antonin Carême devised the first classification of sauces, based on five standard preparations, which he christened 'mother sauces'. These are espagnole (a brown, stock-based sauce thickened with flour and butter), demi-glace (a mixture of espagnole and brown stock that is reduced and usually nowadays thickened by simmering), béchamel (a milk-based white sauce thickened with flour and butter), velouté (a white sauce made with stock rather than milk) and tomato sauce. These five form the base from which all French sauces are derived. They are rarely served in their basic form; instead various ingredients and flavourings are added to make a particular sauce, transforming the original in minutes. The variations are known as 'daughter sauces', for obvious reasons. Over time, the classic French repertoire was expanded by the addition of other sauces introduced from abroad. There is also a separate, smaller category of cold sauces, which are mostly derived from mayonnaise or vinaigrette.

By far the majority of classic sauces are thickened with starch, usually flour. However, during the nouvelle cuisine era of the 1970s, a small group of prominent chefs decided to eliminate starch as far as possible, in order to produce lighter sauces. The heavy, flour-thickened brown sauces were replaced by ones thickened with arrowroot or simply by boiling so that they reduced and thickened naturally. Butter sauces such as beurre blanc were suddenly fashionable, while veloutés became much lighter. This revolutionised sauce-making, and the more time-consuming sauces have never really come back into fashion. For the home cook, this is definitely good news.

So too is the revolution brought about by modern equipment. Blenders and food processors enable anyone to achieve a smooth, shiny, perfectly blended sauce. They have also coincided with the fashion for simple, colourful vegetable and herb purées that can be whizzed up in minutes and served as attractive and wholesome accompaniments to fish and meat.

French culinary traditions die hard, but today sauce-making is a much less structured affair than it used to be. Chefs can pick and choose from a variety of culinary traditions, and it is common to see a juxtaposition of styles and influences on restaurant menus. This in turn influences what we choose to eat at home, and sauce-making for the domestic cook has never been simpler or more accessible.

Author's note Each sauce recipe specifies how much it makes rather than how many people it serves. There is no set portion size with sauces – some people prefer a little; others, like me, enjoy plenty! So do use your own judgement to decide how much you need. All herbs used are fresh unless otherwise stated.

THE BASICS: GETTING STARTED

To make any good sauce, it is vital that you have a good base. This generally entails, in the case of sauce-making, a well-flavoured stock. Stocks are the true foundation of sauces, especially in French cuisine. They are not in themselves difficult to make, but it can be a time-consuming process.

Unfortunately, there are no real shortcuts if you want a really good stock. The supermarket-made varieties sold in cartons are often weak in colour and flavour, and stock cubes are worse still.

I have talked to many home cooks and it is fair to say very few of them make their own stocks. They express difficulty in finding bones, especially veal, game and fish bones; normally chicken bones are the only available option. I urge you to source these more elusive bones by making friends with your butcher and fishmonger, who will get them for you. Failing that, just use chicken bones: you will still achieve far better results than with cubes or store-bought stock.

Here are the basic stocks used throughout the book, which will help you get started on the road to producing great sauces. I find it best not to salt stock, as you might not know what sort of dish it will be used for later, and it is obviously much easier to add salt than take it away.

WHITE CHICKEN STOCK

A light chicken or veal-based stock for soups and light sauces.

makes about 2 litres

2kg chicken carcass or bones (or a mixture of wings, legs and carcass)
3 onions, cut into large chunks
2 large carrots, cut into large chunks
2 sticks of celery, cut into large chunks
2 leeks, white part only, chopped
4 sprigs of flat-leaf parsley
4 sprigs of thyme

1 Remove any skin or obvious excess fat from the chicken. Place it in a large pot, cover with cold water and bring to the boil.

2 Drain the chicken and rinse out the pot. Put the chicken back in the pot and add 3 litres water, to cover.

3 Bring to the boil, then simmer very gently, uncovered, for 1½ hours, skimming off any impurities that form on the surface of the stock from time to time. Add the vegetables and herbs and simmer for a further 1 hour.

4 Strain the stock into a large bowl and leave to cool. It will keep for up to 1 week in the fridge or up to 6 months in the freezer.

WHITE VEAL STOCK

Replace the chicken with an equal weight of veal bones or trimmings, then proceed as for white chicken stock.

DARK CHICKEN, VEAL OR BEEF STOCK

Roasting the meat trimmings and vegetables in the oven gives the stock a darker appearance and a richer, caramelised flavour. Suitable for dark jus-based sauces.

makes about 2 litres

2kg chicken, beef or veal trimmings, cut into large pieces
2 tablespoons vegetable oil
3 onions, cut into large chunks
2 large carrots, cut into large chunks
4 sticks of celery, cut into large chunks
2 leeks, white part only, chopped
4 sprigs of flat-leaf parsley
4 garlic cloves
4 sprigs of thyme
2 tablespoons tomato purée

1 Preheat the oven to 200°C/400°F/gas mark 6. Remove the skin or excess fat from the chicken, beef or veal.

2 Heat the oil in a large roasting tin or ovenproof dish. Add the meat pieces and toss in the hot oil.

3 Place in the oven and roast for 20–30 minutes, until golden all over.

4 Add the vegetables and herbs to the tin, mix them with the browned meat and roast for a further 30 minutes. Stir in the tomato purée and roast for a final 15 minutes.

5 Transfer to a large pot, cover with 3 litres water and bring to the boil on top of the stove. Skim off any impurities that rise to the surface and simmer very gently, uncovered, for 3 hours.

6 Strain and cool, ready for use. This stock will keep for up to 1 week in the fridge or up to 6 months in the freezer.

FISH STOCK

makes about 2 litres

1 tablespoon olive oil
2 onions, peeled and sliced
1 head of fennel, sliced
2 sticks of celery, sliced
1kg fish bones (preferably from white fish), chopped
150ml dry white wine
1 sprig of thyme
1 small bay leaf
2 sprigs of tarragon

1 Heat the oil in a large pan and add the onions, fennel and celery. Cook over a low heat until the vegetables have softened, about 10 minutes.

2 Rinse the fish bones in several changes of water to remove any blood traces, then add them to the pan. Cover and steam for 10 minutes.

3 Add the wine and simmer, uncovered, for 10 minutes.

4 Add the herbs and 2 litres water to cover. Bring to a gentle simmer and cook, uncovered, for 20 minutes. Strain and cool. Fish stock will keep for up to 2 days in the fridge or 1 month in the freezer.

DASHI (ASIAN FISH STOCK)

This is a healthy, fragrant and flavoursome stock, traditionally made from kombu, a brown seaweed native to Japan. You may not be able to find it, but you can find both dried kelp and bonito flakes in oriental stores.

makes about 1 litre

20g dried kelp
20g dried bonito (tuna) flakes

1 Put the kelp into a pan with 1 litre cold water and leave to soak for 3 hours.

2 Bring to the boil and immediately remove the pan from the heat. Add 100ml cold water, then the bonito flakes.

3 Leave to infuse for 15 minutes, then strain through a muslin-lined sieve into a bowl. Dashi will keep for up to 2 days in the fridge or 1 month in the freezer.

VEGETABLE STOCK

Vegetable stocks are wonderful for adding flavour to vegetarian sauces, soups and other dishes. Don't be tempted to use any old vegetables: some work better than others, and making stock is not a way to clear out the fridge or pantry.

makes about 1 litre

3 large carrots, halved lengthways
1 medium celeriac, cut into large chunks
2 sticks of celery, cut into large chunks
2 leeks, white part only, chopped
3 onions, quartered
200g white button mushrooms, halved
1 head of fennel, outer leaves removed, cut into large chunks
3 garlic cloves
4 sprigs of flat-leaf parsley
4 sprigs of thyme

1 Put all the ingredients into a large pot and cover with 2 litres water.

2 Bring to the boil, then simmer, uncovered, for 1 hour. Strain the stock and leave to cool. Vegetable stock will keep for up to 1 week in the fridge or 6 months in the freezer.

DARK VEGETABLE STOCK

For a darker vegetable stock used for making a vegetarian jus, fry all the vegetables and herbs in a little butter and oil with 4 crushed vine tomatoes, then proceed as for the basic vegetable stock.

VARIETIES OF SAUCE

In the overall scheme of successful sauce-making, I think it's vitally important first to come to terms with all the types or varieties of sauce – the sheer scope available to the cook. Sauces fall into two very basic categories, hot and cold, but these can be broken down further as follows:

Emulsified butter sauces Hot white butter sauces, such as beurre blanc or beurre nantais, are traditionally made with a reduction of wine or vinegar with shallots, then emulsified or thickened with butter. Other hot butter sauces include brown butter, drawn butter and noisette butter.

Cold butter sauces are known as compound butters and can be sweet or savoury. These butters are not emulsified, but simply mixed and flavoured with various other ingredients. They are served cold, placed over hot foods to melt on to them.

Pounded purées and coulis The cooked or raw strained purée of fruits such as soft berries, or tomatoes and vegetables, are rubbed through a sieve, then served hot or cold with various dishes. These include pounded sauces made using a mortar and pestle, such as Italian pesto or Asian nam jim.

Emulsified egg-enriched sauces These are rich yet light preparations based on eggs that are either slightly cooked through warming, then thickened with butter (as in hollandaise), or whisked raw, then thickened with oil (as for mayonnaise).

Traditional sabayon sauces (also known by their Italian name of *zabaglione*), made with eggs, wine and sugar, are another form of emulsion sauce, and are especially popular throughout Europe. Crème anglaise (vanilla custard) is also an emulsified sauce, made with egg, milk and cream.

Starch-thickened sauces These sauces are thickened using a roux base (see under *Ways of Thickening Sauces*, below), or by using arrowroot or cornflour. Roux-based sauces include béchamel and velouté. Brown jus sauces tend these days to be thickened with arrowroot (or by natural reduction), to keep them clearer in colour and flavour.

Gravies A gravy is a sauce made from the meat juices left in the pan after roasting or frying. Excess fat is removed from the cooking pan and replaced with wine, stock or even water, which is then simmered vigorously into the caramelised juices. This is known as 'de-glazing'. Sometimes a little flour is mixed with the fat to make a roux and thicken the gravy.

Vinaigrettes and dressings These can be served warm, but are generally used cold to dress salads. They are usually composed of an acid – such as vinegar or lemon – emulsified with an oil base, mustards and various seasonings.

Dipping sauces and salsas A dipping sauce is a common condiment, used to add flavour to a food. Unlike other varieties of sauce, which are applied to the food, the food is put or dipped into the sauce. Dips are traditionally associated with finger foods and are prepared throughout the world, although the most popular originate in Asian and Pacific Rim countries. These include various mayonnaises, guacamole, raita, ketchups, sour-cream dips, Asian fish sauces and barbecue sauces.

Salsas are traditionally associated with Spanish or Latin American cooking; *salsa* is the Spanish word for sauce, and has come to denote a degree of spiciness. They are almost always uncooked (with a few exceptions), and are roundly flavoured with spices in the form of varying heats of chilli and with other aromatic herbs and seasonings.

Ketchups and relishes These usually take the form of preserved sauces, which are, I feel, indispensable to the cook's repertoire. They are available pre-made, but are easy to make at home, can be prepared well in advance, and need no last-minute attention. Ketchup, condiment-style relishes such as horseradish and long-cooked chutneys all fall into this category.

Also included are the Asian and oriental sauces such as soy sauce (made from fermented soya beans) and Thai and Vietnamese fish sauces (from fermented salt-dried fish and shellfish). Chinese sauces include hoisin, oyster sauce, plum sauce and numerous others. Many are used in cooking as well as for a dipping sauce and condiment.

Flavoured syrup sauces Sweet preparations of sugar and water (or fruit juice), cooked until clear and often flavoured with herbs or spices, are easy to make and extremely versatile for desserts.

WAYS OF THICKENING SAUCES

Sauces generally should not be watery in consistency; they can be thickened by one or a combination of the following:

Roux A roux is a mixture of equal parts of melted butter and flour. The two are combined in a pan and cooked to varying degrees, according to the type of roux needed, before the liquid is added. A white roux is cooked just lightly, without browning, as in the case of béchamel.

A blond mix is cooked slowly and for longer, until it is sandy in texture and has a pale biscuit colour; it is used for velouté sauces.

Brown roux is cooked over a gentle heat for longer still, until the flour has turned brown but the butter has not burned. It is traditionally used for demi-glace (half-glaze) sauce (a rich brown sauce used in French cuisine either as a base for other sauces or on its own). However, it is relatively rare these days, even in professional kitchens, where lighter, thickened natural meat stocks, known as *jus lié*, are favoured.

Cornflour and arrowroot need to be 'slaked', which means dissolved, in a little cold water or wine before being added to the hot liquid. They are then stirred in and the sauce thickens almost immediately. This method gives a more refined, clear sauce than thickening with a roux and is particularly popular in Chinese dishes and sweet sauces. As a general guideline, 1 teaspoon slaked cornflour or arrowroot will thicken 200ml sauce. I recommend cornflour for thickening milk and dairy-based sauces and arrowroot for meat sauces, as this adds a superior glossy sheen to the sauce, as well as giving better 'mouth feel'.

Eggs and cream Egg yolks in particular are used as a thickening base of many of the emulsion sauces, such as hollandaise. Egg yolks combined with cream and added to sauces are known as 'liaisons'; these are used to thicken and enrich classic velouté sauces, by being added in the last minute of cooking. Liaisons must be added quickly and while the sauce is off the heat, before being thickened over a low heat. As for custard, it must be stirred constantly until the point where it coats the back of a spoon. The sauce must not boil, or it will curdle, and the sauce will have a scrambled-egg appearance. This thickening method is perhaps the most intimidating for the beginner, and may take a bit of practice. But since today's velouté sauces are made with a cream reduction, rather than with flour, the sauces tend to be rich enough without the need to add a liaison at the end.

Beurre manié (kneaded butter) is a paste-like mixture, made with a ratio of two parts butter to one part flour. It is sometimes also called an 'uncooked roux', the difference being that the butter is not melted as it is for a roux. Beurre manié is added to the hot cooking liquid in small lumps, and whisked evenly for quick thickening.

Butter Chilled butter whisked in small pieces into a hot sauce, off the heat, has a two-tier effect: it gives body and shine to the sauce and acts as a thickener. In the professional kitchen this is known as *monter au beurre*. It can be useful for correcting a sauce that has gone wrong or needs improving (see pages 23 and 30).

Vegetable, fruit and nut purées Many cooked vegetables, fruits and nuts may be puréed to great advantage for use in sauces. Often the resulting sauces can be lighter in texture, prettier in colour and generally more interesting. For example: shallots, mushrooms and potatoes in the Greek potato sauce skordalia; tomatoes in a classic tomato sauce; herbs in an Italian pesto, and nuts for a peanut sauce. Puréeing vegetables and fruits gives a sauce body as well as a silken texture, without the addition of dairy products; it is therefore a useful low-fat and allergy-free option. Generally these sauces are processed in the blender to thicken them, then strained through a fine sieve.

Natural reduction You will notice when making the sauces in this book that it often says 'reduce by half'. This is in fact the simplest technique for thickening a sauce and simply means reducing a thin liquid in quantity by evaporation; the result is a thickened sauce with a more intense flavour.

An open pan over a fairly high heat is the usual way to reduce a sauce. To speed up the process, it can simply be transferred to a larger pan: the greater surface area means evaporation will be faster.

In general, this method is used only when making brown sauces, although some cream-based sauces can be prepared in a similar way. However, cream sauces have a tendency to scorch easily around the edges if they are not monitored regularly as they cook and reduce; the process also needs to be a slower, gentler one.

When reducing any sauce, it is vitally important not to season it, as the flavour will be intensifying as it reduces down, and the results might be too salty. Any impurities that form on the surface need to be skimmed off, to keep the sauce clear and shiny.

Other methods of thickening Bread is sometimes used to thicken a sauce, especially in the Mediterranean region, as in the Catalan romescu sauce, Turkish tarator and Italian agliata, and not forgetting traditional bread sauce (see page 72), served with roasted birds in Britain for centuries.

There are some sauces, traditionally fowl- or game-based ones, that use animal blood as a thickening agent. This is known as a blood liaison, but it is rarely made these days because of restrictions placed on raw blood preparation.

TRICKS OF THE TRADE

In all professions, in addition to technical know-how, there is a handful of useful tricks of the trade, and cooking is no different. Here are some sauce-making tips that I have gained with the experience of many years: over time, they will help you to be more proficient.

THE RIGHT CONSISTENCY

Pouring consistency I always instruct my cooks that a sauce to be served poured over a piece of meat or fish, or as a coating for vegetables, should have a 'pouring consistency'. This simply means it should be thin enough to pour, but not so thin as to be watery. When ready, the sauce should coat the back of a serving spoon lightly, rather than run straight off.

A simple test is to run your finger along the back of the sauce-dipped spoon: if the sauce runs slowly back together, it is ready. This was one of the first things I learnt as a young chef, and I still use it as a guideline to this day.

Coating consistency A sauce that is to cling to the ingredients with which it is served calls for a 'coating consistency', in other words, a slightly thicker consistency than pouring. This could involve anything from saucing a pasta dish, to coating a vegetable with mornay sauce, or other gratin-style dishes. Sauces of this type tend to be based on béchamels or veloutés.

Thick consistency This should be thick enough to bind a mixture for fillings, stuffings or soufflé bases. Again, these are generally béchamel- and velouté-based preparations.

BALANCING OR IMPROVING FLAVOUR

A sauce lacking flavour For brown sauces: add a splash of port or Madeira – it will improve the flavour and colour, providing sweetness and depth.

For white sauces (especially veloutés): add a splash of wine or champagne to fish sauces, and a little port or Madeira to chicken-based veloutés.

Lacking piquancy or bite If a sauce tastes a little dull and flat, a touch of acidity – a squeeze of lemon juice or some wine vinegar – will lift it.

Lacking colour Generally speaking, a sauce lacking in colour means the bones used in the sauce (or for that matter in the base stock) have been inadequately caramelised during roasting. It is vitally important that they, and the vegetables, are cooked to a deep golden brown. Insufficient colouring produces a pale jus. The addition of a tablespoon of soy sauce can help to improve the colour of a sauce.

Too fatty If a sauce appears too fatty, simply add an ice cube and bring it to the boil; you can then ladle off the fat and impurities that rise to the surface.

Too sharp a flavour The addition of a spoonful or two of cream, a little unsalted butter and some sugar, or better still redcurrant jelly, will take an overly sharp edge off a sauce.

Adjusting the seasoning You will see throughout the recipes in the book a note to adjust seasoning at the end of certain recipes. But how do you know what is the correct seasoning? What is too little? What is too much? This knowledge will usually come with experience, although there are a few things to consider in the meantime. Remember too that everyone has a different sense of taste, so what seems like perfection to you may seem bland to someone else.

As a rule, 'adjust seasoning' simply refers to good old salt and pepper. If you like (and it has to be personal) the way a sauce tastes as it is, don't add anything. However, if you think it is missing something, you might need to add a little more of one of the ingredients. For example, sometimes a particular herb is used to accentuate a sauce: if it is not discernible, add a little more.

FINISHING TOUCHES

Below are some tips for balancing certain aspects of the finished sauce. They generally apply to brown sauces, with a few for velouté-based ones.

In professional kitchens, brown sauces are generally finished with small knobs of chilled butter just before serving (the technique called *monter au beurre*). This has a three-tiered effect on your sauce: it lightly thickens it, enriches it and creates a smoother texture. Once the butter is added the sauce should never be reboiled; it will come out of suspension and float on the surface, rendering your sauce somewhat greasy. Cream sauces are also sometimes finished with a little butter, but I find this unnecessary in terms of flavour. The only advantage is that it may add a little extra richness and shine if these are lacking. As well as last-minute butter, sauces are often given a final touch of freshly chopped herbs, which help to finish and enhance the sauce.

Skimming sauces I think of skimming a sauce to keep it clear of foam, fat and impurities as applying a touch of TLC, giving it loving care which will pay dividends to the final result. It is one of the most important, yet overlooked, steps in making fine sauces and soups – and, for that matter, jams. The skimming should take place during the cooking process, any impurities being carefully removed with a small ladle. This will ensure that your sauce does not become cloudy and dull in appearance, but remains clear and shiny. Make it a habit: you will find it improves the general quality of your cooking.

Allowing flavours to develop You will notice with certain sauces, namely salsa and the dipping sauces of Asia, that the recipe often calls for the sauce to be left on hold for a few hours after it is made, to allow flavours to meld together. This ensures that the flavours bloom, that acids calm down and aromatics and spices intensify – so producing a more complex and flavourful sauce.

Fresh and dried herbs and spices I am often asked, can I use dried herbs when making sauces? I have to say that with the exception of dried rosemary, thyme and bay leaves, I have little time for them; I always use fresh herbs in preference. Soft herbs – namely chives, tarragon, basil and coriander – should ideally be chopped at the last minute (or as near to the last minute as possible), then stirred into the finished sauce. A hardy style of herb – such as rosemary or thyme – can be cooked in the sauce.

When using spices, it is best to crush or grind them as they are needed, because they can quickly lose their impact in cooking. One good way to help ensure that you have aromatic herbs and spices is to always buy them in small amounts. Remembering to top them up little and often means you won't have unused quantities turning stale.

MAKING SAUCES AHEAD OF TIME

Although making sauces ahead of time undoubtedly offers a great advantage to any cook, there are certain factors to consider. How to keep a sauce hot, in safe conditions and ready for serving, is the main consideration. Reheating it, and storing it correctly for later use, are other important ones.

Keeping it hot and ready to serve When a sauce is ready, it needs to be kept hot in advance of serving. To do this, I suggest using a bain-marie (water bath). Because the heat is indirect, it is especially good for keeping emulsified sauces warm, such as hollandaise, béarnaise or other butter-based sauces which are less stable than classic white and brown sauces. It is also ideal for keeping other sauces hot.

Place the bowl of (still warm) prepared sauce in a large saucepan, or better still a roasting tin. Add enough hot water to the pan to come up the sides of the bowl and keep it below boiling point. Even if the water in the bain-marie boils, the contents of the sauce bowl will not. A double-boiler saucepan is in effect a bain-marie, and serves the same purpose.

To prevent skin from forming on the surface of your finished sauce, cover it with a piece of lightly buttered greaseproof paper prior to placing it in the bain-marie. I have also discovered over the years that all sauces, but especially emulsified sauces, can successfully be kept warm in a vacuum flask (see Equipment, page 17).

Reheating a sauce Reheating does not mean recooking; it simply means bringing it back to the temperature of the pre-made sauce. For some sauces (cream sauces or white sauces) this needs to be done very slowly, as they tend to burn or scorch easily. Brown sauces, on the other hand, can be brought back to the boil over a high heat.

Storing a finished sauce A sauce you are intending to store should be allowed to cool completely, before being covered with clingfilm, to prevent a skin from forming and to keep it free of any bacterial growth. It should then be put in the fridge, where it will stay fresh and unharmed.

A NOTE ON EQUIPMENT

Pans and frying pans In the French kitchen, copper pans were originally used in classic sauce-making. Nowadays these have been replaced by lighter stainless-steel varieties, which are more commonly used even in the professional environment.

Select various sizes of pans and frying pans, ideally heavy-based and well balanced, as they conduct the heat better. Large pans or stock pots are necessary for making stock in large quantities. Avoid buying cheap aluminium pans, which may react with ingredients such as the acid component of lemons or vinegar.

Non-stick pans have many uses and are especially good for dry-frying spices, so have at least one handy in the kitchen.

A wok is another useful piece of pan equipment, especially when preparing Asian dishes. Woks vary hugely in quality, but it's worth buying a good, sturdy, cast-iron one with a heavy base. Like all cast-iron pans, a wok should not be washed in the conventional way, with detergent, but should be wiped clean, and kept oiled between uses.

Sieves and strainers As with pans, it is handy to keep various sizes of sieve, with different degrees of fineness: some for achieving smooth purées and sauces, and others for clear sauces. The finer your strainer, obviously the more refined your finished sauce will be. In years past, tamis cloth was used to produce the ultimate smooth and glossy sauces, but for exceptionally fine straining this has all but disappeared and been replaced by fine muslin cloth.

Choose stainless-steel sieves and strainers, which do not corrode with time.

Whisks A stainless-steel balloon whisk with a large, firm handle is vital. A selection of sizes will allow you to use one appropriate to the size of your pan, but save the larger ones for whipping egg whites and cream, and choose a smaller one for sauces. Similarly, rotary whisks are fine for beating egg whites or cream, but not for sauce-making.

Small coil whisks seem to be extremely popular these days, and are excellent for small jobs and for getting into the corners of pans while sauce-making. Apart from the practical advantages when making sauces, whisks help to add gloss and shine, especially to white sauces made with stock or milk.

Wooden spoons and spatulas Wooden spoons are best for sauce-making and some other preparations, such as frying, as they do not conduct heat. As well as being cheap and easy to find, they are also the best for use with non-stick frying pans, which are easily scratched.

Spatulas, especially long, flexible ones, are ideal for getting the last bit of food out of pans, and for scraping bowls. A selection of various sizes is handy.

Ladles and skimmers Stainless-steel ladles are very useful for transferring liquids from pan to processor or strainer, and for pushing them through a sieve. Again, having a variety of sizes means you can match them to the job in hand.

Skimmers are like flat, perforated spoons and are generally used to remove fat or other impurities that float to the surface of stocks and sauces.

Blenders and food processors These days blenders can make light work of simple preparations such as pesto. They are also good for breaking down food before it is passed through a sieve to achieve a smoother-textured sauce. It is worth investing in a robust, heavy-duty blender, as it will last much longer than a cheaper version. Hand-held blenders are excellent for puréeing sauces in the pan – especially those in small quantities that would get lost in a jug blender – and take up less storage space. Food processors do the job of the blender, plus much more. With their different blades, they can chop, mix, grate and slice.

In some recipes where the quantities are very small, I advise using a small blender. You can now buy mini blenders to have alongside your larger, jug one, but another good option for small quantities of spice and spice mixtures is to use a small coffee grinder, kept especially for this purpose so that no coffee flavour is imparted.

Graters The easiest way to grate lemon, lime or orange zest is with a fine microplane grater. Unlike with a box grater, the zest doesn't all stick to the grater, you don't grate your fingers, and you can produce fine flecks of zest that more or less dissolve into the sauce you are making. If you buy one with a medium as well as a fine zesting attachment, you will find them endlessly versatile in the kitchen.

Mortars and pestles Before blenders and food processors became the norm, much of the hard work of making puréed sauces was carried out with a mortar and pestle, a versatile duo also used for crushing spices and similar preparations. Many sauces, especially those from Asia, rely on this piece of equipment to make liquid-based sauces, so if you don't already own a mortar and pestle, I would urge you to buy one. Choose a heavy, fairly large one, with a non-reactive surface. In Asia, they are traditionally made of stone or granite, which are much more effective than some glass and wood varieties on the market.

Mixing bowls Again, you want a good selection of stainless-steel bowls, in various sizes. They are ideal for holding strained sauces and for making sauces and dressings. As well as different sizes, choose some that are shallow and some with high sides.

Roasting tins More often used for roasting the bones or vegetables for stock-making, a roasting tin can in fact act as an excellent bain-marie, or water bath, to keep a sauce in another container hot (see page 15).

Measuring jugs These are essential for accurate volume measuring when following a recipe; stainless steel or toughened glass are the best. Plastic jugs have the practical advantage of being lighter and more manageable when full, but they tend to scratch easily, which can make the measurements hard to read.

Vacuum flask You may be surprised to see a vacuum flask as a piece of sauce-making equipment, but I find it useful for keeping all manner of sauces either hot or cold, from a rich brown sauce to a delicate emulsion such as hollandaise or béarnaise. Purchase a well-made, sturdy flask.

STOCKFISH DAUBE
SOUPE AU PISTOU
PATES FRAICHES ou POLENTA
NAPOLITAINE
BOLOGNAISE
PISTOU
DAUBE
GRATIN D'AUBERGINE
45 40 45 60 35 35 35 35 45 45
Lou Pilha Leva
Poivron farci + salade + frites 45
Lasagnes + salade 45
Calamars à la Niçoise 45
Soupe au pistou 35
Ratatouille + salade + frites 40
Jambon + salade + frites 35
Poulet + salade + frites 35
Aïoli (Vendredi) 45
Pâtes fraiches 35
Porchetta + salade frites 45
12

FRENCH classics

It might seem daunting to start this book with the mind-blowing array of classic French sauces. This chapter is inevitably far more regimented than the ones that follow, but all the sauces are well within the grasp of anyone who is prepared to learn a few basics. With practice you will soon feel confident enough to produce them for any occasion.

I have always believed that French cooking owes its fame largely to its wonderful repertoire of sauces. They represent the pinnacle of culinary technique and can transform virtually any dish into something elegant, refined and delicious: think of glorious, golden hollandaise sauce, a smooth, light velouté (the name means 'velvety' in French) or a concentrated, savoury, slow-simmered brown sauce, based on a rich meat stock. I have also included many of my favourite variations on the classic themes – and would encourage you to experiment with other possibilities of your own.

EMULSIFIED SAUCES

Emulsified sauces are sauces that are thickened (or emulsified) with egg yolks and either warm butter (hot emulsions) or oil (cold emulsions).

Chief amongst these sauces are the famous mayonnaise, hollandaise and white butter-based sauces such as beurre blanc. In simple terms, they are formed by an emulsion of fat droplets (butter or oil) combined with a liquid (vinegar, water or stock) and occasionally stabilised with an egg yolk, as in the case of mayonnaise or hollandaise.

These sauces are rich, smooth and luxuriously subtle, but are often thought to be the most intimidating of sauces for beginners to master. Following the instructions to the full, however, will bring success and confidence in time.

PG tip – clarifying butter

Most classic recipes for hollandaise call for clarified butter. It is not essential, but the sauce will be creamier and smoother than if you use just melted butter. To clarify butter, gently melt it in a small pan. Skim the froth from the surface using a small ladle or spoon, then carefully tip the butter into a clean pan or jug, leaving the milky sediment behind. Set aside until tepid and discard the sediment.

Unsalted butter is better for clarifying than salted butter. Clarified butter can be heated to higher temperatures than ordinary butter, making it also ideal for cooking processes such as sautéing.

HOLLANDAISE

Hollandaise sauce as we know it today is the modern descendant of an earlier sauce, believed to have been brought to France by the Huguenots. For me it is the finest of all the warm, emulsified butter sauces – delicious and subtle. ⊕ *It is wonderful served with poached fish, poached eggs and vegetables. The quantities here are enough to sauce 8–10 servings.*

makes 400ml

2 tablespoons white wine vinegar
2 tablespoons water
1 teaspoon lightly crushed white peppercorns
4 free-range egg yolks
250g unsalted butter, clarified (see tip below)
juice of ½ lemon
salt and freshly cracked black pepper
a pinch of cayenne pepper

1 Put the vinegar, water and crushed peppercorns in a small, heavy-based saucepan and bring to the boil. Lower the heat and simmer for 1 minute, or until reduced by one third.

2 Remove from the heat and leave to cool, then strain the liquid into a heatproof bowl. Add the egg yolks to the liquid and whisk together.

3 Set the bowl over a pan of simmering water, with the base of the bowl just above the water. Whisk the mixture for 5–6 minutes, or until it thickens and becomes creamy, smooth and ribbon-like in texture.

4 Slowly add the clarified butter in a thin stream and whisk the sauce until it becomes thick and glossy.

5 Add the lemon juice and season with salt and black pepper and a little cayenne.

6 Serve the sauce immediately or keep it warm in a bain-marie (see page 15) for 15–20 minutes. Putting it into a vacuum flask is also a good way of keeping it warm.

Hollandaise variation

MALTAISE (BLOOD ORANGE) HOLLANDAISE

Replace the lemon juice in the basic hollandaise with the grated zest and juice of 2 blood oranges. I love this sauce with asparagus.

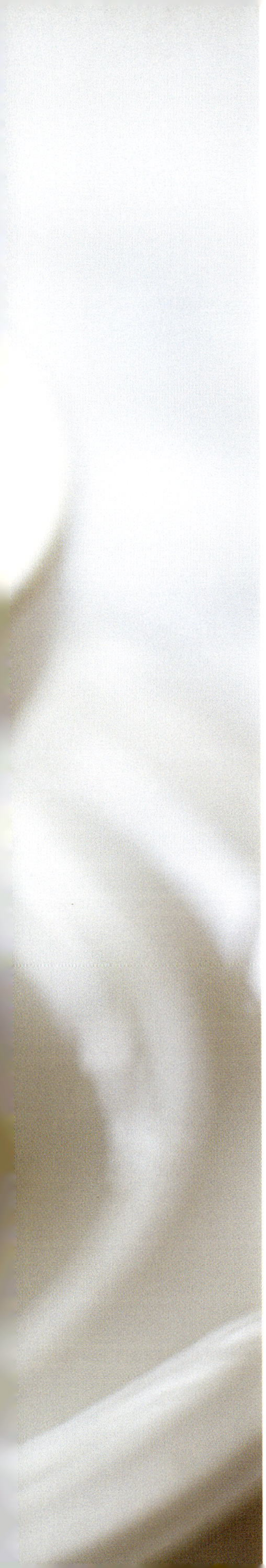

Hollandaise variations

MOUSSELINE HOLLANDAISE

Fold in 75ml lightly whipped double cream just before serving. An ideal accompaniment for hot asparagus or poached fish.

MUSTARD HOLLANDAISE

Add 1 tablespoon Dijon mustard to the finished sauce. Wonderful served with grilled fish, vegetables and chicken.

GINGER HOLLANDAISE

Peel and grate a 2.5cm piece of fresh ginger and heat it with the butter when clarifying, then proceed as for the main recipe. I love this hollandaise, as the ginger adds a lively kick. Ideal with fish or shellfish.

CAVIAR HOLLANDAISE

This and the following sauce are for when you really want to impress. Add 2 tablespoons sevruga caviar to the finished sauce, and serve with poached fish.

BLACK TRUFFLE HOLLANDAISE

Add 1 tablespoon chopped fresh or canned black truffles to the finished sauce. Fantastic with fish, vegetables such as asparagus or artichokes, and poached eggs.

MIXED PEPPERCORN HOLLANDAISE

Add ½ teaspoon each of lightly crushed green and pink peppercorns to the finished sauce. Wonderful with fish, steaks, and duck and lamb cutlets.

BASIL HOLLANDAISE

Add a handful of basil leaves to the finished sauce. Lovely with fish, shellfish such as crab, and egg dishes.

PG tip – repairing a curdled sauce

Emulsified sauces such as hollandaise, béarnaise and cold mayonnaise have a certain notoriety for separating or curdling. If this happens, the problem can be rectified as follows.

Place a fresh egg yolk in a clean bowl with 1 tablespoon water and whisk until combined. Slowly whisk the curdled sauce into the mixture a little at a time, ensuring the 'new' sauce is smooth before you add more of the curdled one. Alternatively, you can whisk iced water or an ice cube into the curdled sauce. In both cases the sauce should return to its emulsified state.

BÉARNAISE

This is essentially a hollandaise sauce made with a reduction of tarragon and shallots. Its unique flavour makes it one of France's most frequently prepared and best-loved sauces. ⊕ *Traditionally served with grilled steak, it is also wonderful with other grilled meats, poultry and fish.*

makes 400ml

15g fresh tarragon
2 shallots, chopped
2 tablespoons white wine vinegar
2 tablespoons water
1 teaspoon lightly crushed white peppercorns
4 free-range egg yolks
250g unsalted butter, clarified (see tip on page 20)
juice of ½ lemon
salt and freshly cracked black pepper
a pinch of cayenne pepper
1 tablespoon chopped chervil leaves

1 Separate the tarragon leaves from the stalks and roughly chop both, keeping them separate. Put the shallots, vinegar, water, crushed peppercorns and tarragon stalks in a small, heavy-based pan and bring to the boil. Lower the heat and reduce the liquid to about 2 tablespoons.

2 Remove from the heat and leave to cool, then strain into a heatproof bowl. Add the egg yolks to the liquid and whisk together.

3 Set the bowl over a pan of simmering water, with the base just above the water. Whisk the mixture for 5–6 minutes, or until it thickens and becomes creamy, smooth and ribbon-like in texture.

4 Slowly add the clarified butter in a thin stream and whisk the sauce until it becomes thick and glossy.

5 Add the lemon juice, season with salt, black pepper and cayenne pepper, then add the tarragon leaves and chervil.

6 Serve the sauce immediately or keep it warm in a bain-marie (see page 15) or vacuum flask.

PG tips

Adding clarified butter
When adding the clarified butter to the eggs in the bowl, you will find it easier if you stabilise the bowl on a dampened tea towel or balance it over the saucepan to keep it from moving as you whisk in the butter.

Repairing a béarnaise
If your béarnaise separates or curdles, follow the tip given on page 23.

Béarnaise variation

RED PEPPER BÉARNAISE

Add 3 tablespoons puréed red pepper (made in a blender) to the finished sauce. Wonderful over a poached egg and with smoked salmon or crab.

Béarnaise variations

SORREL BÉARNAISE

Replace the chervil and tarragon leaves with 20g chopped sorrel leaves in the finished sauce, and omit the tarragon stalks from the vinegar mixture.

MINT BÉARNAISE (paloise)

Replace the tarragon stalks in the main recipe with mint stalks and add 2 tablespoons chopped mint leaves at the end, to replace the tarragon and chervil leaves. Goes extremely well with lamb or duck breast.

TOMATO BÉARNAISE (choron)

Add 2 tablespoons well-reduced tomato sauce or tomato purée to the finished sauce. Fantastic with grilled steak, lamb, chicken and grilled white fish.

CRÈME FRAÎCHE BÉARNAISE

Add a good dollop of crème fraîche to the finished sauce, to lighten it. Wonderful with fish or poached asparagus.

HORSERADISH BÉARNAISE

Add 2 tablespoons creamed horseradish to the finished sauce. You can even serve this with traditional roast beef, although it is especially good with grilled steak or grilled salmon.

PG tip – making sauces in a blender

Most chefs – including myself – even in today's mechanical world, prefer to make their emulsified sauces, such as hollandaise, béarnaise and mayonnaise, by the traditional hand method: that is, a good old bowl and whisk.

This may seem a little unnecessary when a blender does just as good a job and in far less time. It's just a matter of personal taste. In both methods, however, adding the butter or oil too quickly can result in a 'split' or curdled sauce. If this happens, never fear, it can be rectified – don't throw in the towel!

Hollandaise – blender method

Follow the recipe on page 20, but add the cooled, strained vinegar liquid to the blender with the egg yolks and salt and pepper. Blitz for a few seconds until mixed.

With the blender on its maximum speed, trickle in the hot butter via the feed tube and blend until light, thick and fluffy. Add the lemon juice and adjust the seasoning.

Mayonnaise – blender method

Place all the ingredients (see page 30) except the oil and lemon juice in a blender, then blitz for a few seconds. With the blender on its maximum speed, trickle in the oil via the feed tube in a thin, steady stream. Add the lemon juice and adjust the seasoning.

Béarnaise variation

OLIVE BÉARNAISE

Add 2 tablespoons finely chopped pitted black olives to the finished sauce. Particularly good with grilled steaks.

MAYONNAISE

The eggs in mayonnaise hold the oil in suspension, while vinegar and lemon juice add acidity and flavour. It is one of the most loved of all French sauces, especially when served with poached and fried fish dishes and cold meats. As you can see on the following pages, a well-prepared base sauce opens up many possibilities for delicious variations.

Store-bought mayonnaise is fine for some everyday uses, but nothing beats the freshness of homemade. Some chefs also prefer to use a little olive oil in their recipe, but I find this somewhat detracts from the natural flavour, as certain olive oils are strong-tasting and will overpower the sauce.

makes 300ml

2 free-range egg yolks
1 teaspoon Dijon mustard
1 teaspoon white wine vinegar
salt and freshly cracked black pepper
250ml sunflower or rapeseed oil
2 teaspoons lemon juice

1 Ensure that all the ingredients are at room temperature, in particular the eggs and oil: this makes emulsifying easier.
2 Put the egg yolks, mustard and vinegar in a mixing bowl. Add a pinch of salt and pepper.
3 Place the bowl on a dampened tea towel, to keep it steady, and gradually pour in the oil in a thin stream, whisking all the time with the other hand, until it begins to thicken and forms an emulsion.
4 When all the oil has been incorporated and the mayonnaise is thick, stir in the lemon juice and adjust the seasoning to taste.

PG tips

A lighter mayonnaise

For those calorie-conscious amongst you, mayonnaise can be made with whole egg, producing a lighter, less rich and healthier version. And for the cholesterol-aware, rapeseed (otherwise known as canola) oil contains both omega 3 and omega 6 fatty acids and is one of the most heart-healthy oils around. It's being used increasingly in sauce-making.

Repairing a separated mayonnaise

When a mayonnaise separates, it is mainly due to one of the following: either the oil was added too rapidly at the beginning, or the egg or the oil was too cold. Or it may be that the quantity of oil was too great for the amount of egg used. Ensure all ingredients are brought to room temperature before use.

If your sauce does separate for any reason, place an egg yolk and a little mustard in a bowl, then slowly beat in the curdled sauce, adding it a little at a time. If the problem was that the egg and oil were too cold, as mentioned above, whisking in a little boiling water can sometimes restabilise the sauce.

Mayonnaise variation

SEVILLE SAUCE

Finish the basic mayonnaise with orange juice instead of lemon juice and add a little grated orange zest. Particularly good with cold poached asparagus.

Mayonnaise variations

LIGHT MAYONNAISE
Fold 100ml lightly whipped double cream into the basic mayonnaise.

GRIBICHE SAUCE
Use hard-boiled egg yolks, passed through a sieve, instead of raw, then proceed as for the basic recipe. Add 1 tablespoon each of rinsed and chopped capers, chopped chervil and chopped gherkin, with 1 teaspoon Worcestershire sauce, to the finished sauce. Great with fish.

PESTO MAYONNAISE
Add 4 tablespoons pesto (see page 77) to the basic recipe. Particularly good with cold artichokes or as a dip for vegetable crudités.

TYROLIENNE SAUCE
Add 2 tablespoons tomato purée, ½ teaspoon hot chilli sauce and a small quantity of chopped herbs to the basic recipe. Great with fried fish or cold poultry.

AIOLI
Add 4 crushed garlic cloves to the egg yolks at the start, then proceed as for the basic recipe. A little puréed cooked potato may also be added to the egg yolks at this stage. Fantastic for hot or cold fish or as a dip for vegetables, bread and so on.

ROUILLE SAUCE
Add a pinch of saffron threads, 1 teaspoon tomato purée, 1 finely chopped red chilli and ¼ teaspoon cayenne pepper to the basic recipe. Traditionally served with bouillabaisse or other fish soups, but also great with fried fish.

AVOCADO SAUCE
Add to the basic recipe ½ peeled avocado, blended in a food processor with 1 teaspoon lemon juice. Fantastic with cold poached salmon.

FENNEL MAYONNAISE
Add 2 tablespoons chopped fennel fronds, or dill, and 2 teaspoons aniseed liquor, such as Pernod, to the basic recipe.

TARTARE SAUCE
Add to the basic recipe 1 tablespoon each of finely chopped gherkins, rinsed and chopped capers, flat-leaf parsley, chervil and chopped shallots. Traditionally served with deep- or pan-fried fish.

RÉMOULADE SAUCE
Add 1 teaspoon finely chopped tinned anchovy fillet and 2 tablespoons chopped tarragon to the tartare sauce recipe above. Serve with cold meats, cold fish and fried fish.

RED WINE MAYONNAISE
Put 250ml good red wine, a sprig of thyme and a little cracked black pepper in a pan and reduce to a syrup. Add 1 tablespoon redcurrant jelly, strain, then set aside to cool completely. Stir this into the basic mayonnaise recipe and serve with cold meat, especially roast beef.

CURRY MAYONNAISE (sauce indienne)
Add 1 tablespoon mild curry powder to the basic recipe.

THOUSAND ISLAND SAUCE
Add to the basic recipe 3 tablespoons tomato ketchup, 1 tablespoon chopped shallot and ½ tablespoon each of chopped red and green pepper.

GREEN SAUCE (sauce verte)
Put 100g puréed cooked spinach, a bunch of watercress and 1 tablespoon each of chopped chervil, tarragon and chives in a blender. Blitz, then add to the basic recipe.

WARM BUTTER SAUCES

These are also known as white butter sauces or beurre blanc – a hot sauce based on wine and vinegar, reduced with shallots, finished with butter, then whipped until smooth. Traditionally served with fish dishes.

BEURRE BLANC

This is another style of warm, emulsified butter sauce, thought to have come about by accident at the end of the 19th century, when a French cook to the aristocracy forgot to include the eggs in a béarnaise. It is rich in flavour, simple to prepare and stands proudly alongside the other two classic warm butter sauces, hollandaise and béarnaise.

makes 300ml

2 shallots, finely chopped
3 tablespoons white wine vinegar
4 tablespoons dry white wine
2 tablespoons cold water
200g unsalted butter, chilled and diced
salt and freshly cracked black pepper
a squeeze of lemon juice

1 Put the shallots, vinegar and white wine in a small pan and bring to the boil. Lower the heat and reduce for about 2 minutes, to about 1 tablespoon; it should have a syrupy consistency.
2 Over a gentle heat, add the water, then whisk in the butter a little at a time until emulsified.
3 Add salt, pepper and lemon juice to taste. For a smooth sauce, strain it to remove the shallots.

PG tip A dollop or two of double cream added to the wine reduction helps stabilise the sauce if you need to keep it for a length of time, but it does tend to lose some of its buttery flavour.

Variations

NANTAIS BUTTER

This first, often interchangeable, cousin of the beurre blanc sauce is made with equal amounts of wine and wine vinegar, giving the sauce a more acidic flavour. Increase the white wine vinegar in the main recipe to 4 tablespoons and reduce the mixture to 2 tablespoons. Great with oily fish.

BASIL BEURRE BLANC

Add 2 tablespoons chopped basil to the finished sauce.

HERB BEURRE BLANC

A lovely, fresh-tasting sauce. Add 3 tablespoons of your favourite herb: tarragon, chervil and parsley are particularly good.

ROSÉ WINE BEURRE BLANC

The wine adds a lovely red tinge to the butter sauce. Replace the white wine with rosé wine and the vinegar with red wine vinegar. Finish with a spoonful of reduced meat stock (optional).

SOY AND TOMATO BEURRE BLANC

Add 1 tablespoon light soy sauce and 75ml reduced tomato sauce to the reduction before whisking in the butter. Before serving, strain the sauce through a fine sieve. Wonderful with salmon or scallops.

SAFFRON BEURRE BLANC

Add a pinch of saffron threads to the reduction before whisking in the butter, then proceed as for the basic recipe.

GINGER AND LEMON BEURRE BLANC

Add 1 tablespoon grated fresh ginger to the reduction before whisking in the butter, then proceed as for the basic recipe. Finish with 1 teaspoon grated lemon zest. Great with oily fish, such as salmon.

WATERCRESS BEURRE BLANC

Purée a bunch of watercress and add to the finished sauce, then strain it to give a wonderful, green, fresh-tasting butter.

Other warm butter sauces

Below is a list of other simple butter-based sauces on similar lines:

BEURRE NOISETTE (brown butter sauce)

Heat 75g salted butter in a frying pan over a medium-high heat for 1–2 minutes, or until it foams up and becomes golden and nutty brown. Add a squeeze of lemon juice, then pour over pan-fried fish or vegetables.

BEURRE NOIR (black butter sauce)

Prepare as for brown butter sauce (above), but cook the butter for 20–30 seconds longer, or until it takes on a dark colour. Traditionally served with pan-fried skate and capers.

BEURRE FONDU (drawn butter sauce)

Bring 4 tablespoons water to the boil, then whisk in 150g diced, chilled, salted butter until emulsified. Finish with a squeeze of lemon. Most commonly served with asparagus, alongside or instead of hollandaise, it is sometimes also used to reheat vegetables ready for serving.

COMPOUND BUTTERS

Also known as hard butter sauces, these cold, flavoured butter sauces may also be sweetened, to serve over warm desserts (see page 218). Their beauty is that they can be prepared well in advance and kept in the fridge or freezer until needed.

There are some important tips to remember when making these sauces: ensure the butter is at room temperature and soft before beating; ensure the flavouring ingredients are chopped small before adding them to the butter; and finally make sure you allow the butter to stand for 30 minutes prior to rolling in the paper, to allow the flavours to permeate.

MAÎTRE D'HÔTEL BUTTER (parsley butter)

⊕ *The most popular of the cold butter sauces, served with grilled fish, steaks or vegetables.* For a variation, you can replace the parsley with other herbs of your choice, such as tarragon, basil or thyme.

200g good-quality unsalted butter, softened
salt and freshly cracked black pepper
a pinch of paprika
3 tablespoons chopped flat-leaf parsley
juice of ¼ lemon

1 Put the softened butter in a bowl and season with salt, pepper and paprika.
2 Add the parsley and lemon juice and beat together well.
3 Leave to stand for 30 minutes, then roll the butter in greaseproof paper or foil into a sausage shape, twist the ends and tighten to form a bon-bon shape. Chill in the fridge or freezer until needed.
4 To serve, remove the butter from its paper roll, leave to soften slightly for 2–3 minutes, then cut into slices about 1.5cm thick. Place the butter on your piece of cooked meat or fish and it will melt slowly over the food – delicious!

Variations

SHELLFISH BUTTER

Substitute 125g finely chopped peeled cooked prawns, shelled cooked lobster or crayfish for the parsley. Mix in 1 teaspoon tomato purée, a good dash of cognac and the juice of another ¼ lemon. Great with fish and shellfish.

MERLOT BUTTER

Put 100ml good merlot wine and a finely chopped shallot in a pan and reduce to 2 tablespoons. Add to the butter in place of the paprika, parsley and lemon juice. Wonderful with grilled steaks.

ROQUEFORT BUTTER

Add 50g crumbled Roquefort cheese in place of the paprika, parsley and lemon juice. Ideal with grilled steak and lamb or pork chops.

PORCINI BUTTER

Soak 10g dried porcini mushrooms in 160ml water and 50ml Madeira for 1 hour. Place in a pan, simmer for 5 minutes, then remove the mushrooms and leave them to cool. Reduce the liquid to a syrup, strain and leave to cool. Chop the mushrooms finely and add them with the reduced liquid to the butter in the main recipe, in place of the paprika, parsley and lemon juice.

ESCARGOT BUTTER

Add 1 teaspoon crushed garlic, use only 2 tablespoons parsley and omit the paprika and lemon juice. Traditionally served with snails, vegetables or grilled meats. You can try smoked garlic here for an interesting variation.

FOIE GRAS BUTTER

Add 50g puréed foie gras pâté and 2 tablespoons Madeira in place of the paprika, parsley and lemon juice. Good with grilled meats and game.

SMOKED PAPRIKA BUTTER

Add 1 teaspoon smoked paprika to the butter in place of the parsley and lemon juice. Wonderful with grilled meats and fish.

CAFÉ DE PARIS BUTTER

Replace the parsley and lemon juice with 2 tablespoons tomato ketchup, 1 teaspoon Dijon mustard, ½ teaspoon chopped rinsed capers, 1 chopped shallot, 2 finely chopped, rinsed tinned anchovy fillets and 1 teaspoon each of chives and tarragon. Mix well, then stir in a dash of Madeira or cognac. Great with grilled meats.

GRAINY MUSTARD BUTTER

Add 1 teaspoon grainy mustard in place of the paprika and lemon juice, using just 2 tablespoons parsley. Goes well with grilled fish, seafood and meat, and game dishes.

FENNEL AND SAFFRON BUTTER

Infuse a good pinch of saffron threads in 4 tablespoons water. Add this to the butter in the basic recipe with ½ teaspoon toasted fennel seeds in place of the paprika, parsley and lemon juice. Wonderful with seafood, especially scallops.

STEAK BUTTER

Replace the parsley and lemon juice with 4 very finely chopped tinned anchovies or 1 teaspoon anchovy paste. Traditionally served as an accompaniment to steaks in gentlemen's clubs.

WHITE SAUCES

Béchamel is the name for the classic white sauce made from milk and a white-based roux. It forms the base of many great sauces, such as the famous cheese sauce, mornay. When correctly made, a good béchamel will be smooth and creamy in appearance, rather than thick and pasty. Like many of the great French classic sauces, béchamel is often replaced in restaurant kitchens nowadays by a sauce made completely of rich cream, and sometimes a classically made béchamel is finished with a spoonful or two of cream.

BÉCHAMEL

The onion studded with cloves adds extra flavour to the milk base.

makes 600ml

1 small onion, halved
4 whole cloves
600ml full-fat milk
1 small bay leaf
45g unsalted butter
45g plain flour
a little salt and freshly cracked black pepper
a little freshly grated nutmeg
60ml double cream (optional)

1 Stud each onion half with 2 cloves, then place in a pan with the milk and bay leaf. Bring to the boil and simmer gently for 4–5 minutes, to infuse.

2 In another pan, melt the butter, add the flour and cook for 30–40 seconds, stirring frequently with a wooden spoon, until the roux is pale yellow.

3 Strain the milk through a fine strainer, then beat it vigorously into the roux, until the sauce is smooth and silky in appearance.

4 Slowly bring the béchamel to the boil, reduce the heat, then simmer for 20 minutes, beating occasionally, until the sauce is smooth and glossy.

5 Season with salt, pepper and nutmeg and stir in the cream, if using.

PG tip If you are in a hurry, you can adopt the all-in-one method: do not infuse the milk, but instead put all the ingredients (omitting the onion, cloves and bay leaf) in a pan over a low heat and stir continuously until the sauce boils and thickens. Keep stirring for 3–4 minutes. Season with salt, pepper and nutmeg, and add the cream, if using.

Béchamel variations

MORNAY SAUCE (cheese sauce)

Classically made with Gruyère or another Swiss cheese, this is great for coating vegetables such as cauliflower, leeks and broccoli. Simply add 100g grated Gruyère or Cheddar and 1 teaspoon Dijon mustard to the finished sauce, off the heat. Stir in 2 free-range egg yolks mixed with 4 tablespoons lightly whipped double cream.

EGG AND MUSTARD SAUCE

Add 2 teaspoons Dijon mustard and 2 tablespoons each of single cream, roughly chopped hard-boiled free-range eggs and roughly chopped flat-leaf parsley to the finished sauce. Lovely served over poached fish, especially haddock or plaice.

CAPER SAUCE

Add 50g well-rinsed and roughly chopped superfine capers and the juice of ¼ lemon to the finished sauce. Great with a boiled leg of lamb or mutton. If you are serving it with this, add 150ml of the poaching lamb liquor as well.

SOUBISE SAUCE

Blanch 2 chopped large onions or 4 chopped shallots in boiling water for 2 minutes, then drain and sauté in 50g unsalted butter until very soft but not browned. Add these to the basic sauce recipe with a pinch of sugar and cook, stirring, for 15–20 minutes. Blitz in a blender until smooth, then stir in 100ml double cream. Superb with lamb or pork.

GOOSEBERRY SAUCE

This sauce I first came across as a trainee in the West Country: a local classic served with grilled mackerel, it remains one of my favourites to this day. Poach 100g fresh gooseberries in 100ml water with 2 tablespoons granulated sugar for 15 minutes, then add the béchamel from the basic recipe and cook for 2–3 minutes. Transfer to a blender and blitz until smooth and creamy, or use a stick blender.

VELOUTÉ

Made in the same way as béchamel, velouté is a smooth, velvety sauce made using a white roux and a flavoured white stock (veal, chicken or fish). It is vitally important that the stock is of the highest quality, to obtain the best results. Many chefs have abandoned the classic velouté in favour of a sauce made from stock with reduced cream and flavourings, as a matter of convenience and flavour. Below are recipes for both versions.

CLASSIC VELOUTÉ

makes 600ml

1 litre well-flavoured chicken, veal or fish stock (see pages 8–9)
60g unsalted butter
60g plain flour
salt and freshly cracked black pepper

1 Bring the stock to the boil. In another pan, melt the butter, add the flour and stir to make a white roux.
2 Stir in the stock with a wooden spoon, then change to a whisk and bring the mixture to the boil. Skim off any impurities that form on the surface.
3 Simmer over a low heat until reduced by one third, then strain.

MODERN VELOUTÉ

The reduction of wine, along with the aromatics, produces a richer sauce than the classic version given on the left.

makes 600ml

4 shallots, chopped
a little fresh thyme if using chicken or veal stock, or 100g chopped button mushrooms if using fish
15g unsalted butter
300ml dry white wine
400ml well-flavoured chicken, veal or fish stock (see pages 8–9)
375ml double cream

1 In a pan, sweat the shallots and thyme or mushrooms in the butter until softened. Add the wine and bring to the boil.
2 Reduce the heat and simmer for 20–25 minutes, or until the liquid has reduced by two thirds and is syrupy in consistency.
3 Add the stock, return the mixture to the boil and cook over a high heat for a further 20 minutes, or until reduced by half. Add the cream, return it to the boil, then lower the heat and simmer until it has reduced by half again; it should have thickened enough to coat the back of a spoon. Strain the sauce before using.

Velouté variations

Choose your type of stock to match the dish you are serving.

AURORE (tomato velouté)

Add 100ml fresh tomato sauce (see page 58) or passata to the finished sauce. Great with poached chicken, crab or lobster.

HERB VELOUTÉ

Add 2 tablespoons of your favourite herb to the finished sauce; I like a mixture of chervil, tarragon and chives. Lovely with poached fish, shellfish and white meat dishes.

ANCHOVY AND MUSTARD VELOUTÉ

Add 1 teaspoon Dijon mustard and 1 teaspoon anchovy essence to the finished sauce. Good with poached fish, especially sole or halibut.

WILD MUSHROOM VELOUTÉ

Add 75g sautéed wild mushrooms to the finished sauce, or 10g dried mushrooms presoaked in water for 1 hour, drained and added to the basic sauce along with the soaking liquid. If you prefer a smooth sauce, transfer the sauce to a blender and blitz until smooth.

SHELLFISH VELOUTÉ

Velouté can also be made using the cooking juices of poached shellfish such as mussels or clams instead of the stock. The shellfish is generally added to the sauce to serve.

Velouté variation

SAFFRON VELOUTÉ

Add a good pinch of saffron threads to 4 tablespoons boiling stock or water, then add to the finished sauce. Serve with fish or shellfish, such as poached scallops – delicious! I often also add some chopped tomato and basil.

BROWN SAUCES

LIGHTLY THICKENED VEAL JUS

In days gone by, this brown sauce was known as a 'demi-glace' (half glaze) – once the mainstay of classic French cuisine. It took the best part of two days to prepare, and formed the base of many of the famous classic brown sauces. Today it has all but vanished in favour of a lighter sauce called a 'jus' (juices). This jus can be made with meat, poultry, game, fish and vegetables and produces a clearer, more refined and certainly less time-consuming sauce. It should be thick and glossy, and should lightly coat the back of a spoon.

makes 600ml

- 3 tablespoons vegetable oil
- 350g veal trimmings
- 150g chicken wings, roughly chopped into small pieces
- 4 shallots, chopped
- 100g mushrooms or mushroom trimmings and peelings
- 1 carrot, roughly chopped
- 1 garlic clove, crushed
- ½ tablespoon tomato purée
- a small sprig of thyme
- 1 small bay leaf
- 300ml dry white wine
- 600ml water
- 1.5 litres veal, beef or dark chicken stock (see page 9)
- 1 tablespoon arrowroot, mixed with a little water

PG tip As veal can be hard to obtain as well as expensive, beef trimmings can be used instead.

1 Heat the oil in a large pan and, when it is very hot, add the meat pieces. Fry over a high heat for about 20 minutes, moving the pieces around until they are golden brown all over.

2 Add the vegetables and garlic and continue to fry for a further 10 minutes, until golden and caramelised. Add the tomato purée, thyme and bay leaf, and cook for a further 2–3 minutes.

3 Add the wine and water and bring to the boil, scraping the sediment from the pan with a wooden spoon to release the caramelised juices.

4 Cook, uncovered, for 20 minutes, to reduce by two thirds. Add the stock and return to the boil, then simmer for 20–25 minutes to reduce by half again, skimming to remove any impurities.

5 Stir in the arrowroot and mix to thicken the liquid. Cook for 2 minutes, then strain through a fine sieve.

LIGHTLY THICKENED POULTRY JUS

Follow the recipe above for lightly thickened veal jus, but substitute chicken wings or duck bones for the veal trimmings. Made this way, it is light and delicate – perfect for chicken dishes or braising vegetables. The jus-based sauces below are ideally made with a base of veal jus, but chicken can be used if preferred.

Jus-based brown sauces

BORDELAISE SAUCE

One of the great French sauces for sautéed steaks or roast beef joints. Place 3 finely chopped shallots, 250ml red wine, a sprig of thyme, 6 crushed black peppercorns and a small bay leaf in a pan, bring to the boil and reduce by half. Add 300ml jus, then simmer, uncovered, for 10 minutes. Strain through a fine sieve, then add 50g cleaned bone marrow (soaked in warm water for 5 minutes). Drain, whisk in a knob of chilled butter and season to taste.

Brown sauce variation

DEVILLED SAUCE

Bring 3 chopped shallots, 6 crushed black peppercorns, 1 bay leaf, a sprig of thyme, 100ml dry white wine and 75ml white wine vinegar to the boil. Reduce by half, add 300ml veal jus and simmer, uncovered, for 10 minutes. Strain, stir in 1 tablespoon Worcestershire sauce and a knob of chilled butter, then season to taste. Great with grilled chicken or calves' liver.

CHATEAUBRIAND SAUCE

Another great steak-inspired sauce. Cook 3 chopped shallots, a few mushroom trimmings, a little thyme and 1 bay leaf in butter until golden. Add 100ml dry white wine, then simmer, uncovered, for 10 minutes. Add 200ml jus and cook for a further 5 minutes. Strain through a fine sieve. Reheat to serve, then whisk in 50g maître d'hôtel butter (page 36) and 1 tablespoon tarragon. Season to taste.

ROBERT SAUCE

One of the greats; the mustard adds a real kick. It is traditionally served with pork, but I enjoy it with chicken too. Or for a variation, also good with pork, add some finely chopped gherkins to create sauce charcutière. Heat 1 tablespoon unsalted butter in a small pan, add 1 small onion, finely chopped, and cook over a low heat for 8–10 minutes, until cooked but not coloured. Pour in 100ml dry white wine and 2 tablespoons white wine vinegar and reduce by half. Add 300ml jus and cook for 15 minutes. Strain, pressing down on the onions for maximum flavour. Heat the mixture, stir in 3 teaspoons Dijon mustard and another tablespoon of butter, season to taste and serve.

POIVRADE SAUCE

A light, peppery-flavoured sauce. Sweat 1 crushed garlic clove, 1 chopped shallot, 1 chopped small carrot and 1 chopped stick of celery in 10g unsalted butter. Add 200ml red wine, 75ml red wine vinegar, a sprig of thyme and 1 small bay leaf, and cook, uncovered, for 10 minutes. Add 12 lightly crushed black peppercorns and 200ml veal jus and simmer for 5 minutes, then strain through a fine sieve. Whisk in a good knob of chilled butter and season to taste.

REFORM SAUCE

Perhaps my all-time favourite: I love its hot and sweet flavour. Sweat 2 chopped shallots in a little butter, add 150ml red wine and reduce by half. Add 200ml jus and reduce by half again. Stir in 2 tablespoons redcurrant jelly, strain, whisk in a knob of chilled butter and season to taste. Serve with lamb cutlets cooked in a crispy crumb crust.

TAPENADE

Wonderful with lamb or duck breast. Sweat some shallots in a little butter. Add 100ml dry white wine and cook, uncovered, for 5 minutes. Add 250ml veal jus and cook for 10 minutes. Add 2 tablespoons tapenade (see page 74), whisk in a good knob of chilled butter, then season to taste.

FORTIFIED WINE-BASED JUS

Heat 200ml prepared jus with 100ml Madeira, port or Marsala. Cook for 5 minutes, then whisk in a good knob of chilled butter and season to taste.

PÉRIGOURDINE SAUCE

For real extravagance, heat 150ml Madeira-fortified jus (see above), then add 1 tablespoon chopped fresh or canned truffles. Simmer for 2–3 minutes, whisk in a knob of butter and season to taste.

GAME JUS

This hearty sauce is used as a base sauce for furred and feathered game dishes. Although it is fair to say that most people do not prepare game at home, I thought it worthwhile including it here anyway, for the few who do.

makes 750ml

2 tablespoons vegetable oil
750g game trimmings, cut into small pieces
25g unsalted butter
2 carrots, chopped
1 onion, chopped
a sprig of thyme
1 bay leaf
10 black peppercorns, lightly crushed
2 tablespoons red wine vinegar
20g plain flour
150ml red wine
600ml game or veal stock (see page 9)
600ml water
½ teaspoon juniper berries

1 Heat the oil in a large, heavy-based pan. Add the game trimmings and fry until golden, about 20 minutes. Add the butter, vegetables, herbs and peppercorns, and fry until caramelised.
2 Add the vinegar and heat for 1 minute. Add the flour, mix well and cook over a low heat for 5 minutes. Pour in the wine, stock and water, then bring to the boil, skimming off any impurities that rise to the surface.
3 Add the juniper berries and simmer, uncovered, for 45 minutes, skimming regularly. Strain through a fine sieve.

Variations

The very traditional sauces below are variations on the above game jus, and follow classic French principles. They have a great affinity with strong, rich game such as venison or hare.

GAME POIVRADE SAUCE

Put 4 tablespoons redcurrant jelly with 1 tablespoon crushed black peppercorns and 100ml red wine in a pan. Cook over a moderate heat until reduced and syrupy, about 3–4 minutes. Add the game jus and strain, then finish with 100ml port.

GRAND-VENEUR SAUCE

Follow the poivrade recipe above, but add 100ml double cream and a knob of unsalted butter with the port and whisk into the sauce before serving.

SALMIS SAUCE

For a wonderfully rich and caramelised flavour, add 100ml truffle juice and 150ml good-quality sherry to the finished game jus.

PAN SAUCES AND GRAVIES

Pan sauces are in essence one of the simplest ways available to the cook for making a sauce. They are made from the caramelised juices left behind by pan-fried meat, poultry or fish, and you make the sauce there and then in the pan, while the meat is resting somewhere else. This method of sauce-making it known as 'deglazing', which simply means the pan juices are swilled with a liquid – usually wine, stock, cream or meat jus – to dislodge any caramelised pieces.

Gravies are made from the meat juices left in a pan after roasting or frying. Any excess fat is normally removed before wine or stock is added. Sometimes flour is mixed into the fat and browned for a few minutes before the liquid is added, resulting in a thicker gravy. Some chefs thicken their gravies by adding a little beurre manié (see page 12), or by reducing the stock down in the pan until it thickens naturally.

Here are a few of my favourite pan sauce and gravy recipes.

SAUTÉED CORN-FED CHICKEN CHASSEUR

serves 4

2 tablespoons vegetable oil
15g unsalted butter
1 corn-fed chicken, about 1.5kg, cut into joints
salt and freshly cracked black pepper
100ml dry white wine
100g button mushrooms, sliced
400g tin tomatoes, chopped
2 tablespoons chopped tarragon leaves
150ml lightly thickened chicken jus (see page 44)

1 Heat the oil and butter in a heavy-based frying pan. Season the chicken pieces liberally with salt and pepper and add them to the pan.
2 Fry the chicken until golden all over and cooked through, about 8–10 minutes. Remove to a plate and keep warm.
3 Deglaze the pan with the wine and boil for 1 minute, stirring up the caramelised cooking juices, before adding the mushrooms, tomatoes and tarragon.
4 Cook for 5 minutes to infuse the flavours. Add the chicken jus to the pan and cook for a further 2 minutes.
5 Pour over the chicken and serve.

ENTRECÔTE 'BALSAMIC AU POIVRE'

A little balsamic vinegar added to the classic version of steak au poivre produces something a bit different.

serves 4

1 teaspoon black peppercorns, lightly crushed
2 teaspoons drained green peppercorns in brine, rinsed
4 entrecôte (sirloin) steaks, 200g each
2 tablespoons vegetable oil
15g unsalted butter
1 tablespoon balsamic vinegar
2 tablespoons brandy
100ml lightly thickened veal jus (see page 44)
50ml double cream
salt and freshly cracked black pepper

1 Mix the black and green peppercorns together and lightly press them on to the surface of both sides of the steaks.
2 Heat the oil and butter in a heavy-based frying pan and add the steaks. Cook them on both sides to your liking: 2–3 minutes each side for rare; 4–5 minutes each side for medium, and 7–8 minutes per side for well-done. Remove to a plate, cover with foil and keep warm.
3 Deglaze the pan with the balsamic vinegar and brandy and simmer for 1 minute, stirring up the caramelised cooking juices as the liquid reduces.
4 Add the veal jus and cream and cook for 2–3 minutes, until the sauce is thick enough to coat the back of a spoon.
5 Season with salt and pepper, then pour over the steaks and serve.

CALVES' LIVER VÉNITIENNE

⊕ *This sauce is good not only with offal but delicious with pork and beef too, or served over creamy mashed potatoes.*

serves 4

2 tablespoons vegetable oil
25g unsalted butter
8 thin slices of calves' liver, 90g each
1 onion, very thinly sliced
8 sage leaves, roughly chopped
90ml dry white wine
60ml Marsala
100ml lightly thickened veal jus (see page 44)
salt and freshly cracked black pepper

1 Heat the oil with 15g of the butter in a heavy frying pan. When it is very hot, add the liver slices, in batches, and fry for 2½ minutes on each side. Remove to a plate, cover with foil and keep warm.
2 Add the onion and sage and fry until the onion is lightly golden and softened, about 3–4 minutes.
3 Deglaze the pan with the wine, stirring up the caramelised cooking juices.
4 Add the Marsala and veal jus and boil for 2–3 minutes. Season to taste, then whisk the remaining butter into the sauce and serve poured over the liver.

BASIC ROAST GRAVIES

This recipe is suitable for any roasted joint, whether meat, poultry or game. Ideally you should use the appropriate stock for enhancing the gravy: lamb stock for roast lamb, chicken stock for roast chicken and so on.

makes 600ml

25g plain flour
600ml well-flavoured hot stock, the type according to the roast (see page 9)
salt and freshly cracked black pepper

1 After roasting the joint, remove to a warmed plate and set aside to rest. Remove the excess fat from the roasting tin, leaving approximately 2 tablespoons.
2 Over the heat, and using a wooden spoon, scrape up the caramelised pan juices, then add the flour, blending it well into the fat and juices.
3 Cook for 2 minutes until the flour becomes a light golden colour.
4 Add the stock and bring to the boil, stirring constantly. Boil until the sauce thickens and is reduced by a third.
5 Season to taste, then strain through a fine sieve and serve.

Variations

HERB AND MUSTARD GRAVY

Simply add a small handful of your favourite herbs to the reducing gravy, such as rosemary, thyme or sage. Whisk in 1 tablespoon Dijon mustard before straining.

WINE-INFUSED GRAVY

Substitute 100ml red wine, port or white wine for 100ml of the stock and add gradually as for the stock.

BEER GRAVY

Add a bottle of dark beer to the gravy in place of the same volume of stock. Wonderful with roast beef or pork.

VEGETABLE-BASED SAUCES

Vegetable sauces add not only colour to a dish but a touch of freshness as well – ideal for vegetarian (using vegetable stock, of course) and light dishes. This type of sauce, which derives its body either entirely or in part from puréed vegetables, is often referred to as a coulis (see also fruit coulis, page 211). As a rough guide, the quantities here are generally enough for eight servings, although this will depend on how you are using each one, and with what.

SWEET PEPPER SAUCE

⊕ *Great with steamed fish, pasta and vegetables.*

makes 450ml

2 red, green or yellow peppers, deseeded and chopped
45g unsalted butter
a generous pinch of sugar
200ml vegetable stock (see page 10) or water
a sprig of thyme
100ml double cream
salt and freshly cracked black pepper

1 Put the chopped peppers in a pan with 15g of the butter and the sugar.

2 Cover with a lid and sweat over a low heat until the peppers begin to soften. Add the stock or water and thyme and bring to the boil.

3 Reduce the heat, then simmer gently, uncovered, for 15–20 minutes.

4 Discard the thyme and transfer the mixture to a blender. Blitz to a purée, then strain back into the pan through a fine sieve.

5 Reheat the sauce and whisk in the cream and remaining butter. Season to taste.

GARDEN PEA AND MINT SAUCE

⊕ *Great with poached salmon or poached or steamed asparagus. It is also very good over goat's cheese ravioli. For a variation, you can replace the mint with basil.*

makes 450ml

300ml white chicken or vegetable stock (see pages 8 and 10)
150g podded fresh peas (or frozen)
a small handful of mint leaves
60ml single cream
10g unsalted butter
salt and freshly cracked black pepper

1 Put the stock in a pan and bring to the boil. Add the peas and mint leaves and return to the boil.

2 Cook for 5–6 minutes for fresh peas, 2 minutes for frozen peas, then transfer the mixture to a blender. Blitz until smooth, then strain back into the pan through a fine sieve.

3 Reheat the sauce and add the cream. Whisk in the butter and season to taste.

PUMPKIN SAUCE

I had to include this sauce as it is so good served with seasonal wild mushrooms or with pasta. A must for the autumn season.

makes 750ml

2 tablespoons olive oil
30g unsalted butter
350g peeled and deseeded pumpkin, cut into 1.5cm pieces
2 shallots, finely chopped
1 garlic clove, crushed
500ml light chicken or vegetable stock (see pages 8 and 10)
100ml single cream
a pinch of ground cinnamon
salt and freshly cracked black pepper

1 Heat the oil and 20g of the butter in a pan, add the pumpkin pieces and cover. Cook for 5 minutes over a medium heat, until softened and lightly caramelised.

2 Add the shallots and garlic and cook for a further 2–3 minutes.

3 Add the stock and boil for 8–10 minutes.

4 Transfer the mixture to a blender and blitz until smooth. Strain back into the pan through a fine sieve.

5 Whisk in the cream and remaining butter and bring to the boil, still whisking. Add the cinnamon and season with salt and pepper.

SHALLOT TARTS WITH WILD MUSHROOMS AND PUMPKIN SAUCE

serves 4

350g small shallots
150g sugar
30g unsalted butter
100ml sherry vinegar
½ teaspoon thyme leaves
350g prepared puff pastry (fresh or frozen), thinly rolled
225g selection of wild mushrooms
2 tablespoons olive oil
salt and freshly cracked black pepper
½ quantity of pumpkin sauce (see left), heated

1 Blanch the shallots in boiling water for 4–5 minutes, then drain and leave to cool.

2 Put the sugar in a non-stick frying pan and heat, stirring constantly until the sugar caramelises.

3 Add 20g of the butter and stir into the caramel.

4 Add the blanched shallots, sherry vinegar and thyme and continue cooking until the caramel completely coats the shallots and the shallots are soft and cooked through. Transfer to a bowl and leave to cool.

5 Preheat the oven to 180°C/350°F/gas mark 4. When the shallot mixture is cool, divide it between 4 tart tins, 9–10cm in diameter, and place on a baking sheet.

6 Stamp out 4 discs, 9–10cm in diameter, from the pastry and lay over each shallot-filled tin, pressing around the edges to seal.

7 Melt the remaining butter and brush the pastry tops. Transfer to the oven and bake for 15–20 minutes.

8 Meanwhile, sauté the mushrooms in a hot pan with the olive oil, then season well and keep warm.

9 Turn out the tarts, shallot-side up, on to 4 serving plates. Top each with the wild mushrooms, pour the pumpkin sauce around them and serve.

PORCINI CREAM SAUCE

If you wish to use fresh porcini, replace the dried with 175g washed and chopped fresh ones, cooked in a little butter at the beginning of the recipe.

⊕ *Great with veal or chicken, or added to a mushroom risotto, gnocchi or pasta.*

makes 300ml

10g dried porcini mushrooms
150ml hot chicken or vegetable stock (see pages 8 and 10)
25g unsalted butter
2 shallots, chopped
50ml port
50ml Madeira
60ml double cream
3 tablespoons lightly thickened chicken jus (see page 44; optional)
salt and freshly cracked black pepper

1 Soak the porcini in the stock for 30 minutes, then strain, reserving the soaking liquid and the porcini separately.

2 Heat 10g of the butter in a pan and add the soaked porcini and shallots. Cover and sweat for 5 minutes over a low heat.

3 Add the port, Madeira and reserved stock and bring to the boil. Cook for 2–3 minutes.

4 Transfer the mixture to a blender and blitz until smooth, then strain back into the pan through a fine sieve.

5 Add the cream and chicken jus, if using, and cook for 3–4 minutes. Whisk in the remaining butter, season to taste and serve.

ASPARAGUS AND LEMON SAUCE

⊕ *I often add 1–2 chopped sticks of lemon grass, to the stock, with the asparagus peelings. With or without this addition, the sauce is wonderful served with fish or shellfish, such as lobster or scallops, or with buttered baby leeks and morels.*

makes 450ml

300g asparagus spears, trimmed (keep the trimmings) and chopped
250ml white chicken or vegetable stock (see pages 8 and 10)
20g unsalted butter
60ml double cream
½ teaspoon finely grated lemon zest
salt and freshly cracked black pepper

1 Put the asparagus trimmings in a pan with the stock and simmer for 10–15 minutes to infuse, then strain, reserving only the stock.

2 Heat half the butter in a pan, then add the asparagus and cook, covered, for 5 minutes.

3 Add the infused stock and boil for 5–8 minutes until the asparagus is soft.

4 Add the cream and cook for a further 2 minutes. Transfer to a blender and blitz until smooth

5 Strain the sauce back into the pan through a fine sieve and, over the heat, whisk in the remaining butter and the lemon zest. Season to taste.

MISCELLANEOUS SAUCES

An independent group of sauces that form the basis of many great dishes in French cuisine.

RED-WINE-FLAVOURED FISH JUS

This sauce has something of the professional kitchen about it, but is easy to make at home.

⊕ *It's lovely with pan-roasted fish or used as a base to braise firm-fleshed fish, such as monkfish.*

makes 600ml

50g chilled unsalted butter
4 shallots, roughly chopped
150g button mushrooms or mushroom trimmings
1 bay leaf
a sprig of thyme
600g white fish bones (sole, monkfish or halibut), chopped
400ml full-bodied red wine (Barolo is particularly good)
100ml port
250ml chicken or veal stock (see page 9)
45ml double cream

PG tip Some chefs finish the sauce, as I occasionally do, by turning the remaining butter into a noisette butter (see page 35), which is whisked into the sauce after the cream. I find it gives the sauce a more rounded flavour, but either way is equally delicious.

1 Heat 25g of the butter in a large, heavy-based pan, then add the shallots, mushrooms, bay leaf and thyme. Cook for 4–5 minutes until the vegetables are lightly golden.

2 Place the fish bones on top of the vegetables, cover and cook for 2–3 minutes.

3 Add the wine and simmer, uncovered, for 5 minutes.

4 Add the port and stock and bring to the boil. Reduce the heat and simmer gently for a further 25 minutes.

5 Strain through a fine sieve into another pan and bring to the boil.

6 Add the cream and the remaining butter, cut into small pieces, and whisk until smooth.

Variations

CORIANDER RED WINE JUS

A wonderful sauce to accompany meaty fish such as sea bass, halibut or turbot. At the end, simply add 2 tablespoons chopped coriander and cook it in the sauce for 1 minute to infuse the flavours.

Alternatively, replace the coriander with another herb of your choice – tarragon and flat-leaf parsley are particularly good.

ANCHOVY FISH JUS

The anchovy flavour makes this a lovely accompaniment for sole or turbot. Add 1 teaspoon anchovy essence to the finished sauce.

GRAIN MUSTARD AND BALSAMIC JUS

Add 2 teaspoons balsamic vinegar and 1 teaspoon Pommery grain mustard to the sauce at the end of cooking. Wonderful with white fish, roasted or grilled.

VEGETARIAN JUS

This sauce has opened up many new possibilities for the vegetarian cook and has really evolved only with the rise in popularity of vegetarian cuisine over the last 10–15 years. Optimal caramelising of the vegetables is vital to bring out the natural flavours, and at the same time to enrich the colour and appearance of the sauce.

makes 1 litre

2 tablespoons vegetable oil
4 shallots, chopped
150g carrots, roughly chopped
50g celery, roughly chopped
2 garlic cloves, crushed
a pinch of sugar
200g mushrooms or mushrooms trimmings, chopped
4 ripe tomatoes, chopped
1 tablespoon tomato purée or passata
2 sprigs of thyme
1.5 litres dark vegetable stock (see page 10)
100ml Madeira
45ml port
1 tablespoon light soy sauce
20g arrowroot, mixed with a little water

1 Heat the oil in a large pan and add the shallots, carrots, celery, garlic and sugar. Fry over a moderately high heat until the vegetables are golden, about 15 minutes.

2 Add the mushrooms and fry for 3–4 minutes until golden. Add the tomatoes, purée and thyme and cook, covered, for 5 minutes.

3 Add the stock and bring to the boil. Skim off any impurities and simmer for 15 minutes.

4 Add the Madeira, port and soy sauce and simmer for a further 30 minutes.

5 Add the arrowroot, to thicken the sauce slightly, then strain through a fine sieve.

Variations

WILD MUSHROOM AND TRUFFLE JUS

For a richer mushroomy sauce, replace the mushrooms with 20g dried wild mushrooms, soaked in water for 20 minutes, then proceed as for the basic recipe. At the end, finish the strained sauce by whisking in 2 teaspoons truffle oil and 10g butter.

LIQUORICE JUS

An unusual sauce which I love spooned over a creamy risotto of cauliflower or butternut squash. Add 2 tablespoons chopped chewy soft liquorice along with the wines and soy sauce, then proceed as for the basic recipe.

BOUILLABAISSE-STYLE JUS

Created along the lines of the famous Provençale fish sauce or soup, this is particularly good served with green vegetables such as spinach, asparagus, leeks or braised fennel. Replace the mushrooms with 2 chopped red peppers.

LENTIL AND TOMATO SAUCE

A rich, earthy-flavoured sauce, wonderful with stuffed vegetables such as rice-filled aubergines. Add 100g soaked puy lentils, 2 tablespoons balsamic vinegar and 200g chopped tomatoes at the same time as the stock, then proceed as for the basic recipe.

TOMATO SAUCE

Tomatoes are world food; you will find them in almost every section of this book. This tomato sauce is a simple yet extremely effective and versatile sauce for any cook. Unlike its more rustic Sicilian cousin (see page 87), it has a smooth finish.

Do not be tempted to blitz the finished sauce in a blender or food processor, as the sauce can lose its wonderful rich red colour. When your tomatoes are not as ripe or red as you would like, which can generally be the case except during the summer months, don't be afraid to replace them with good-quality tinned varieties. In fact, most Italian chefs and cooks prefer to use these as good-quality tinned often offer excellent flavour and colour, something that fresh tomatoes cannot always do.

makes 1 litre

15g unsalted butter
4 tablespoons olive oil
2 shallots (or 1 large onion), chopped
a sprig of thyme
1 small bay leaf
3 garlic cloves, crushed
1kg overripe vine plum tomatoes (preferably San Marzano), deseeded and chopped (or 2 x 400g tins)
2 tablespoons tomato purée
1 tablespoon caster sugar
100ml tomato juice (optional)
salt and freshly cracked black pepper

1 Put the butter and oil in a pan and add the shallots, thyme, bay leaf and garlic. Sweat over a low heat until the shallots are softened and translucent.
2 Add the tomatoes, purée, sugar and tomato juice, if using. Bring to the boil, then reduce the heat and simmer, uncovered, for 20–25 minutes.
3 Use a ladle to press the sauce through a fine sieve. Season to taste.

Variation

ROASTED TOMATO SAUCE

Use only fresh tomatoes for this. Cut the tomatoes in half, rub each with a little of the garlic and place on a baking tray. Drizzle over the olive oil, sprinkle over the thyme leaves and place on a baking tray. Season lightly with salt and pepper and roast in a preheated oven at 120°C/250°F/gas mark ½ for 40 minutes, until the tomatoes are very soft. Add the roasted tomatoes to the recipe as in step 2 of the basic recipe, left, and proceed as described there.

RAW TOMATO SAUCE

For me, this can be made successfully only during the hot summer months when the vine-ripened tomatoes are succulent and sweet-tasting. A food mill or ricer-style strainer gives the best results, but a blender is also fine. ⊕ *This sauce is beautiful served with pasta, fish and shellfish.*

makes 500ml

450g overripe vine plum tomatoes (preferably San Marzano), chopped
1 tablespoon tomato purée
10 basil leaves
1 tablespoon caster sugar
2 tablespoons sherry, or raspberry, vinegar
100ml olive oil
salt and freshly cracked black pepper

1 In a bowl, combine the tomatoes, purée, basil, sugar and vinegar. Cover and leave at room temperature for 2 hours.
2 Purée the mixture by putting it through a food mill (or blender) to form a smooth sauce.
3 Whisk in the oil, season to taste and serve at room temperature. The sauce is best used quickly, while super-fresh tasting.

SAUCE AMÉRICAINE

This shellfish sauce uses the carcass shells of lobster, prawns or crab and results in a wonderful cream-based sauce for fish dishes.

makes 1 litre

75g unsalted butter
500g lobster, prawn or crab shells, broken up into small pieces
1 stick of celery, finely chopped
1 carrot, finely chopped
1 onion, finely chopped
2 garlic cloves, crushed
100ml brandy
75g plain flour
150ml dry white wine
6 large tomatoes, roughly chopped
3 tablespoons tomato purée
10g tarragon leaves
1 litre fish (or chicken) stock (see pages 8 and 9)
8 white peppercorns, crushed
100ml double cream

1 Heat the butter in a large, heavy-based pan and add the shells. Fry for 2–3 minutes.

2 Add the chopped vegetables and garlic, and cook for a further 5 minutes. Add the brandy and cook for 1 minute.

3 Add the flour and make a roux around the shells and vegetables. Cook for 2–3 minutes, then add the wine and cook for 2–3 minutes.

4 Stir in the tomatoes, purée, tarragon and stock, and bring to the boil, stirring.

5 Add the peppercorns and simmer for 40 minutes over a low heat, skimming off any impurities that rise to the surface.

6 In a separate pan, boil the cream, then stir it into the sauce. Strain through a fine sieve.

VINAIGRETTES AND DRESSINGS

A cold, emulsified sauce, vinaigrette is also known as a salad dressing, and is one of the simplest of cold sauces to make. I always have a batch of classic vinaigrette in my fridge: it not only brings a salad to life, but also forms the base flavour.

For a good vinaigrette, I insist on two things: top-quality vinegar, such as white wine, Champagne, sherry, red wine or balsamic, along with a mixture of a mild-tasting olive oil and a non-scented oil. In general, a ratio of three to four parts oil to one part vinegar will produce a very acceptable vinaigrette.

I include here my favourite classic vinaigrette recipe along with a few well-tested variations.

CLASSIC VINAIGRETTE

makes 150ml

2 teaspoons Dijon mustard
2 tablespoons good-quality red wine vinegar (cabernet sauvignon)
salt and freshly cracked black pepper
65ml vegetable or sunflower oil
65ml mild olive oil

1 In a bowl, mix the mustard and vinegar with some salt and pepper.
2 Gradually add in the oils one at a time, in a thin stream, whisking constantly, until emulsified. Check the seasoning.

PG tip There are some interesting smoked olive oils entering the marketplace at the moment and I believe they will become more popular in future, so watch out for them. A smoked olive oil in classic vinaigrette will add an interesting smoky overtone to a salad.

Variations

GARLIC VINAIGRETTE

Add 1 finely crushed garlic clove to the bowl with the salt and pepper. Proceed as for the basic recipe, then leave to stand for 1 hour before using to allow the flavours to infuse.

NUT OIL VINAIGRETTE

Use sherry vinegar instead of wine vinegar and replace the olive oil with hazelnut or walnut oil. Proceed as for the basic recipe. Fantastic on a salad of crispy leaves with grilled goat's cheese.

RAVIGOTE VINAIGRETTE

Add to the basic vinaigrette 1 tablespoon each of chopped roasted peppers, capers, gherkins, hard-boiled eggs, flat-leaf parsley and shallots. Great with grilled fish, artichokes, asparagus and smoked fish.

NIÇOISE VINAIGRETTE

Add to the basic vinaigrette the zest of ¼ lemon, 1 tablespoon each of chopped capers, black olives and chopped basil, 2 finely chopped tinned anchovy fillets and 2 deseeded, chopped ripe tomatoes. Great with grilled leeks, asparagus, grilled fish and shellfish, or over baked feta or goat's cheese.

ANISEED VINAIGRETTE

Adds a wonderful hint of liquorice to the dressing. Put 1 shallot, 1 crushed garlic clove and 1 teaspoon green peppercorns in a blender and blitz with the basic vinaigrette until fine. Transfer to a bowl and add 1 teaspoon lemon zest, a pinch of ground aniseed and 1 tablespoon Pernod. Leave for 1 hour to infuse before using. Wonderful added to chopped salad greens to accompany scallops or duck breasts.

CITRUS VINAIGRETTE

Add the juice and zest of 1 lime or lemon to the basic vinaigrette, with ½ teaspoon sugar.

HONEY MUSTARD VINAIGRETTE

In a pan, heat 1 tablespoon grainy mustard and 2 tablespoons runny honey. Add the warm mixture to the basic vinaigrette.

HERB-INFUSED VINAIGRETTE

Add 1 teaspoon each of chopped chervil, tarragon, chives, parsley and mint to the basic vinaigrette; alternatively, choose a single variety of herb.

TOFU BALSAMIC VINAIGRETTE

Put 50g silken tofu, 1 crushed garlic clove, 1 tablespoon chopped fresh coriander and 4 tablespoons water in a blender and blitz until smooth. Add to the basic vinaigrette made with good-quality balsamic vinegar (aged if possible).

CARAMELISED SQUASH AND ICED GOAT'S CHEESE SALAD

It is important to use a firm cheese for this dish, which means choosing a mature variety such as crottin de Chavignol.

serves 4

1 tablespoon olive oil
10g unsalted butter
1 butternut squash, peeled, deseeded and cut into 2.5cm pieces
6 rashers of streaky bacon, cut into pieces
a small handful of walnut halves
salt and freshly cracked black pepper
4 tablespoons honey mustard vinaigrette (see above)
a good bunch of watercress, trimmed
1 firm goat's cheese, about 80g, frozen

1 Heat the oil and butter in a large frying pan and when it is hot add the squash and fry until golden, about 3–4 minutes.
2 Add the bacon and walnuts and toss together. Continue cooking until the squash is just tender and retaining its shape. Season with salt and pepper.
3 Add the vinaigrette and heat for 1 minute.
4 Transfer the squash to a plate and scatter over the watercress.
5 Remove the goat's cheese from the freezer and finely grate it over the salad. Serve immediately.

CREAMY VINAIGRETTES

Vinaigrettes are delicious when made into creamy-style dressings, with the addition of a little light cream, yoghurt, mayonnaise, soft cheeses or curd cheese. Here are a few of my favourites:

ROQUEFORT DRESSING

Put 75g Roquefort (or another blue cheese of your choice) in a blender with 90ml single cream, 2 teaspoons sherry vinegar and 4 tablespoons olive oil. Blitz until smooth with 2 tablespoons warm water.

WHITE SOFT CHEESE DRESSING

In a pan, gently heat 50ml cream almost to the boil, then add 100g ripe Camembert, Brie or a soft goat's cheese. Remove from the heat and stir until melted. Set aside to cool, then add to the basic vinaigrette.

WARM, COOKED SALAD DRESSINGS

Warm salad dressings are great during the summer months for those who enjoy light sauces with their food. They are particularly good with fish and shellfish as well as grilled poultry. They can be prepared in advance and reheated slowly.

SAUCE VIERGE

⊕ *A warm dressing for fish or shellfish, with provençale overtones.*

makes 150ml

90ml extra virgin olive oil
1 garlic clove, crushed
2 small tinned anchovy fillets in oil, drained and finely diced (optional)
2 plum tomatoes, deseeded and cut into small dice
juice of ½ lemon
2 tablespoons chopped basil
1 tablespoon chopped flat-leaf parsley
salt and freshly cracked black pepper

1 Warm the oil and garlic in a small pan, then add the anchovies, if using, and tomatoes. Warm gently for 2 minutes to infuse the flavours and soften the tomatoes.

2 Stir in the lemon juice and herbs and season to taste.

Variations

SAUCE ANTIBOISE

Another provençale sauce, first discovered in the port of Antibes. Replace the basil and parsley in sauce vierge, left, with fresh coriander leaves, and add ½ teaspoon toasted and lightly cracked coriander seeds to the warmed oil and garlic at the beginning of the recipe.

ORANGE AND GREEN PEPPERCORN SAUCE

Heat 4 tablespoons olive oil in a pan and add 1 chopped shallot and 1 crushed garlic clove. Cook until softened. Add 100ml fresh or concentrated orange juice and whisk until amalgamated. Add 1 teaspoon green peppercorns and season to taste. Great poured over pan-fried fish, such as skate or cod.

Kunstgen
Handarb
JOHANNES KRUG · NÜ

EUROPE and the mediterranean

The sauces of this region encompass a wide variety of styles and flavourings, but they all share a sense of appropriateness to the climate and country to which they belong. The light, fragrant avgolémono of Greece, made with egg and lemon, is perfectly refreshing on a hot day; the robust, warming horseradish creams of Germany, served with smoked fish and meats, are ideally suited to a cold climate; while the fiery piri piri of Portugal and romescu of Spain are designed to cool you down in sweltering temperatures. In Italy you can even track the changes in climate and agriculture from north to south by the style of its regional sauces – from robust meat ragús or cream sauces in the cooler, dairy-loving north all the way down to the tomato- and olive-oil-based sauces of the arid south. The UK has perhaps the least clearly defined culinary profile of any European country, yet its sauces have a character all of their own: well-loved favourites such as bread sauce with poultry and mint sauce with lamb date back to medieval times and are a vital part of the culinary landscape.

SAVOURY FRUIT SAUCES

Most of the traditional savoury fruit sauces we still enjoy in Britain today, such as apple or gooseberry, date back to the 15th century. Research shows that in those days they tended to be sweeter and almost always spiced. Modern sauces have evolved into a more sweet-savoury affair. The majority of fruit sauces are quick and uncomplicated preparations, the fruit cooked in a sweet syrup and simply served with roasted meats and game. The recipes below make enough for about eight servings.

PEAR SAUCE

⊕ *This is a medieval recipe I have used for years and is great with roast duck, or spread on toast for breakfast.*

makes 600ml

450g ripe but firm pears, peeled, cored and cut into pieces
1 teaspoon ground cinnamon
1 pared strip of lemon rind
25g granulated sugar
75ml water

1 Put the pears, cinnamon, lemon rind and sugar in a pan. Bring to the boil, lower the heat and cook until the pears have softened.

2 Transfer to a blender and blitz to a purée. Serve warm or cold.

APPLE SAUCE

Use tart Bramley cooking apples for best results.

makes 600ml

400g apples, peeled, cored and thickly sliced
100ml water
25g granulated sugar
juice of 1 lemon
25g unsalted butter

1 Put the apple pieces in a pan with the water, sugar and lemon juice and bring to the boil.

2 Simmer for 10–12 minutes or until the apples have softened.

3 Leave to cool, then pass through a fine sieve, or purée in a blender.

4 Return to the heat, stir in the butter and serve warm.

SPICY CRANBERRY SAUCE

⊕ *It's a terrible waste to save this tart fruit sauce for the Christmas turkey, as it's also very good with duck, game, roast ham and cold meats.*

makes 600ml

450g fresh or frozen cranberries
200g demerara sugar
finely grated zest of 1 and juice of 2 oranges
½ teaspoon ground mixed spice

1 Put all the ingredients in a pan and bring slowly to the boil, stirring until the sugar has dissolved. Lower the heat and simmer for 30 minutes until the berries are very soft. Serve warm or at room temperature.

QUINCE SAUCE

Quinces are not always easy to come by and take a long time to cook, but they are really worth the trouble. ⊕ *Great with game and especially roast pork.*

makes 600ml

400g firm quinces, peeled
100ml water
225g granulated sugar
1 teaspoon finely grated lemon zest

1 Using a very good, heavy knife, cut the quinces into pieces, removing the cores, and put in a pan with the remaining ingredients.
2 Cook gently over a low heat for up to 1¼ hours, until dark amber in colour. Purée in a blender.

GOOSEBERRY SAUCE

⊕ *A lovely, seasonal fruit sauce: tart in flavour and wonderful with oily fish and roast pork.*

makes 600ml

400g fresh or frozen gooseberries
100ml water
100g granulated sugar
25g unsalted butter

1 Put the gooseberries in a pan with the water and half the sugar and bring to the boil. Reduce the heat and simmer for 10–15 minutes, until softened.
2 Transfer to a blender and blitz to a purée, then add the remaining sugar.
3 Return to the pan to heat through. Stir in the butter and serve warm.

Variation

Add some freshly chopped mint leaves to the finished sauce.

CUMBERLAND SAUCE

Purists may be surprised to see a variation of this classic fruit sauce flavoured with blueberry jam (see page 71), rather than redcurrant jelly. I tried it one Christmas served with beautifully sliced gammon when I didn't have any redcurrant jelly, and I found I actually preferred the blueberry version, as did my guests. ⊕ *Both versions are wonderful served with cold turkey, duck or goose.*

makes 300ml

grated zest and juice of 1 small orange
grated zest and juice of 1 lemon
250g redcurrant jelly
1 teaspoon Dijon mustard
75ml port
½ teaspoon ground ginger
1 large shallot, finely chopped
salt and freshly cracked black pepper

1 Put the orange and lemon zest in a small saucepan of boiling water. Boil for 2 minutes, then drain and set aside.
2 Put the redcurrant jelly, mustard and port into a pan and mix. Add the ginger and gently heat until the jam melts, but do not boil.
3 Add the orange and lemon juice, the drained zest and the shallot. Season to taste and serve at room temperature.

Cumberland sauce variation

BLUEBERRY CUMBERLAND SAUCE

Replace the redcurrant jelly with 250g blueberry jam.

OLD-FASHIONED BREAD SAUCE

Roasted game and fowl in season would not be complete without this creamy and delicately spiced bread sauce. The addition of a little double cream and butter enriches it beautifully.

makes 600ml

1 onion, cut in half
4 cloves
450ml full-fat milk
4 tablespoons double cream
75g fresh white breadcrumbs
25g chilled unsalted butter, cut into small pieces
salt and freshly cracked black pepper
freshly grated nutmeg

1 Stud the onion halves with the cloves and put in a pan with the milk and 2 tablespoons of the cream. Bring gently to the boil, then remove from the heat and leave to infuse for 10 minutes.
2 Strain the milk into a clean pan and reheat almost to boiling point, then whisk in the breadcrumbs and cook for 2 minutes, until the sauce thickens.
3 Add the remaining cream and stir in the chilled butter pieces.
4 Season with salt, pepper and nutmeg to taste.

PG tip Bread sauce must be made when needed, kept warm and served immediately, as it doesn't take kindly to reheating.

MINT SAUCE

Traditionally served with roast or grilled lamb, mint sauce, with its pungent piquant flavour, is the perfect foil for the rich, fatty-tasting meat.

makes 150ml

100g mint leaves
2 tablespoons caster sugar
2 tablespoons malt vinegar, or to taste

1 Using a mortar and pestle, crush the mint leaves and sugar to a coarse pulp. Set aside for 30 minutes to allow the sugar to draw the juices from the mint.
2 Stir in the vinegar, to taste.

Variation

BALSAMIC MINT SAUCE

Replace the malt vinegar with sweet-tasting balsamic vinegar.

GERMAN HORSERADISH SAUCE

In Britain we prefer our horseradish sauce mixed with cream – to accompany one of our natural treasures, roast beef – but it can be omitted to create a sharper, or German, version. Always use fresh, crisp horseradish, as it loses its strong flavour the older it gets. ⊕ *Delicious with smoked fish.*

makes 200ml

1 fresh horseradish root, about 350g
juice of ½ lemon
a good pinch of sugar
a pinch of salt
150ml semi-whipped cream (optional)

1 Peel the horseradish and grate it finely into a bowl. Take care as the fumes can be extremely strong.

2 Add the lemon juice, sugar and salt to taste.

3 Stir in the semi-whipped cream, if using. Cover with clingfilm and refrigerate until ready to use.

Variation

CHRAIN

Chrain is a sauce synonymous with Jewish cooking, traditionally served with smoked fish. Add 2 tablespoons natural yoghurt and 2 finely grated raw beetroots to the basic sauce.

PG tip A good way to protect your face from the eye-watering pungency of horseradish is to cover your nose with a paint mask.

SMOKED EEL WITH POTATO, ASPARAGUS AND HORSERADISH VINAIGRETTE

serves 4

12 asparagus spears, trimmed
8 quails' eggs
30g rocket
30g curly endive
15g chervil sprigs
4 skinless smoked eel fillets, 300g each, cut into 5cm lengths
1 sweet dill pickled cucumber, sliced
300g cooked new potatoes, thinly sliced

for the horseradish vinaigrette

½ teaspoon horseradish sauce (see left)
75ml olive oil
1 tablespoon chopped flat-leaf parsley
1 teaspoon white wine vinegar

1 Make the vinaigrette by placing all the ingredients in a bowl and whisking until amalgamated.

2 Cook the asparagus in boiling, salted water for 2 minutes, then remove to iced water to refresh. Drain and dry.

3 Hard-boil the quails' eggs for 3 minutes, then remove to iced water. Peel and cut each in half.

4 Toss the rocket, endive and chervil together in a bowl, then divide between 4 serving plates.

5 Place the eel fillets on the salad leaves, with the halved eggs and sliced pickle.

6 Put the potatoes and asparagus tips in a bowl, pour in a little horseradish vinaigrette and toss to coat. Scatter over the salad, drizzle over any remaining dressing and serve.

TAPENADE

One of the classic French provençale sauces, tapenade takes its name from the dialect word *tapeno*, meaning caper, which may seem a little strange given that the dominant ingredient of the dish is the wonderful niçoise black olive, so synonymous with the area. Tapenade can be kept in a sealed jar in the fridge for up to 3–4 months.

makes 300ml

100g good-quality pitted black olives
6 tinned anchovy fillets in oil, drained
50g capers, drained and rinsed
3 garlic cloves, crushed
150ml olive oil
freshly cracked black pepper

1 Put the olives, anchovies, capers and garlic in a blender and pulse 3–4 times, until coarsely chopped.

2 Using the feeder tube, with the motor running, add the oil in a thin stream.

3 Transfer to a bowl and add some black pepper.

Variation

TOMATO TAPENADE

Replace the olives with sun-blush tomatoes and 1 teaspoon each of thyme leaves and chopped rosemary. Proceed as for the main recipe.

PG tip Use either version of the tapenade as a pungent sauce to enliven sandwiches, goat's cheese, grilled meats or fish.

PROVENÇALE TOASTS WITH SEA BASS AND TAPENADE

serves 4

4 slices of good-quality country-style bread, about 2.5cm thick, or 8 slices of baguette, cut diagonally, about 1.5cm thick
4 tablespoons extra virgin olive oil
4 small fillets of sea bass, about 120g each, cleaned
salt and freshly cracked black pepper
2 garlic cloves
2 tablespoons chopped herbes de Provence (basil, chervil, rosemary and parsley)
100ml tapenade (see left)

1 Heat a grill pan over a high heat. Brush both sides of the bread with olive oil.

2 Grill the bread until lightly charred, about 1 minute per side. Remove and keep warm. Meanwhile, season the sea bass liberally with salt and pepper.

3 Add the fish to the grill pan and cook for 2–3 minutes on each side.

4 Rub the hot grilled toasts with the garlic and a little more oil, and sprinkle with the herbs.

5 Place a grilled piece of sea bass on each piece of toast (cut each piece of fish in half if you are using the smaller slices of baguette). Top with a dollop of tapenade and serve immediately.

PESTO

As a bit of a traditionalist, I make my pesto by using a mortar and pestle to pound the ingredients before adding the oil, but in this modern world a blender does a quicker and equally successful job. It will keep in the fridge for 2–3 days before losing its vibrant colour and freshness.

makes 150ml

75g basil leaves
2 garlic cloves, chopped
1 tablespoon roughly chopped pine nuts
2 tablespoons finely grated Parmesan cheese (preferably Reggiano)
100ml extra virgin olive oil
salt and freshly cracked black pepper

1 Put the basil, garlic, pine nuts and Parmesan in a blender. With the motor running, slowly pour in the oil in a thin stream through the feeder tube, and process until smooth.

2 Add salt and pepper to taste, transfer to a bowl (or container with a lid), cover and refrigerate until needed.

PG tip You can replace the basil with another favourite herb: flat-leaf parsley, coriander or mint, for example. Or try one of the variations on this page.

Variations

PUMPKIN SEED AND GOAT'S CHEESE PESTO

Replace the pine nuts with 250g pumpkin seeds, baked in a moderate oven (190°C/375°F/gas mark 5) for 10 minutes until lightly golden and fragrant, then cooled. Replace the basil with 50g mint, and use 50g soft goat's cheese instead of the Parmesan. Proceed as for the basic recipe.

ASPARAGUS PESTO

Trim and remove the woody ends of 8 asparagus spears and cook in boiling, salted water for 2 minutes. Refresh in iced water to stop them cooking further, then dry them well with a cloth. Cut the asparagus into small pieces and add to the blender with the other ingredients in the main recipe. Serve with either pasta or grilled fish.

ROCKET PESTO

Replace the basil with rocket leaves for a hotter pesto.

RAPINI PESTO (BROCCOLI RABE)

This pesto is served warm, tossed with pasta. Cook 150g broccoli spears in boiling water, until very soft. Drain well, put in a blender and blitz until coarsely puréed. Add all the ingredients from the main recipe and blitz again for 10 seconds.

HAZELNUT PESTO

Replace the pine nuts with 3 tablespoons chopped hazelnuts. Omit the Parmesan and add ½ teaspoon hot chilli flakes instead.

TROFIE TRAPENESE STYLE

This is a Sicilian pasta dish that blends tomatoes into the pesto, and uses local almonds instead of pine nuts.

serves 4

50g whole almonds
2 garlic cloves, crushed
1 small red chilli with seeds, finely chopped
salt and freshly cracked black pepper
20g mint leaves, preferably spearmint
50g basil leaves
30g pecorino cheese (or Reggiano Parmesan)
100ml extra virgin olive oil
3 large, ripe but firm tomatoes, peeled and cut into small dice
450g trofie pasta (or bucatini or fusilli)

1 Put the almonds, garlic, chilli and a little salt and pepper in a blender. Blitz until everything is very roughly chopped.
2 Add the mint, basil, cheese and oil and blitz again until the herbs are chopped and the mixture is blended. The texture should be chunky, not puréed.
3 Transfer to a bowl, toss in the tomatoes and adjust the seasoning.
4 Cook the pasta in a large pan of boiling, salted water, until just cooked, or *al dente*.
5 Drain the pasta, toss with the sauce and serve immediately.

FONDUTA

Often confused with the classic Swiss fondue, fonduta is a similar sauce from Italy's Piedmont region. Fontina is the cheese of choice, although it can successfully be made with other cheeses, such as Gruyère, Emmenthal or even Dutch Edam – anything rich and creamy. ⊕ *For a real treat, scatter some freshly shaved white truffles over the top. One of the nicest dishes I have ever tasted in Italy was in Sicily where fonduta was served over some simple poached eggs, with the shaved white truffle on top – highly recommended!*

makes 600ml

350g fontina cheese, cut into small cubes
1 teaspoon cornflour
600ml full-fat milk
salt and freshly cracked black pepper
4 free-range eggs, beaten
75g unsalted butter, cut into small cubes

1 Put the cheese, cornflour and milk in a small pan with a little salt and pepper. Place over a low heat, stirring constantly, until the cheese has melted. It will become a little stringy.
2 Beat the eggs and butter in vigorously and continue cooking over a low heat until the sauce becomes runny, creamy and smooth.
3 Pour into bowls or ramekins and serve immediately with chunks of crusty bread.

Variation

Add 2 tablespoons grappa to the finished fonduta: lovely with chicken.

SALSA VERDE

(Italian green sauce)

Salsa verde is a rustic sauce, served cold, and is different all over Italy. Some versions include bread soaked in vinegar, some have chopped egg – the variations are endless. ⊕ *Used as a condiment for meat, fish, poultry and vegetable dishes, for me it's the greatest sauce in Italian cookery.*

makes 300ml

1 garlic clove
30g flat-leaf parsley, leaves only, roughly chopped
10g mint leaves, roughly chopped
4 tinned anchovy fillets in oil, drained
1 teaspoon Dijon mustard
20g sweet dill-pickled gherkins
50g superfine capers in brine, drained and rinsed
2 tablespoons white wine vinegar
120ml extra virgin olive oil
salt and freshly cracked black pepper

1 Crush the garlic with a mortar and pestle, then add the herbs and anchovy fillets. Crush to a pulp.
2 Add the mustard, gherkins and capers, then crush to a purée-like consistency.
3 Add the vinegar, then slowly drizzle in the olive oil to form a semi-fluid sauce. Season to taste and serve. Salsa verde will keep in a sealed container in the fridge for 2–3 days.

ROAST PORK BELLY WITH BLACK CABBAGE AND SALSA VERDE

⊕ *Delicious with mashed potatoes finished with olive oil rather than butter.*

serves 4

1kg piece of boneless pork belly
salt and freshly cracked black pepper
2 teaspoons fennel seeds
4 tablespoons olive oil
400ml dry white wine
600ml veal or chicken stock (see pages 8 and 9)
1 large cavolo nero (black cabbage) or Savoy cabbage, about 600g
1 onion, finely chopped
1 garlic clove, crushed
100ml water
150ml salsa verde (see left), to serve

1 Preheat the oven to 220°C/425°F/gas mark 7. Cut the pork into 4 equal-sized slabs and rub with salt, pepper and fennel seeds. Place in a shallow roasting tin, drizzle over half the oil and put into the oven for 20–25 minutes, to start off the crackling.
2 Remove the pork from the oven and turn down to 180°C/350°F/gas mark 4. Pour the wine and stock around the pork. Return to the oven to cook for a further 1–1¼ hours, or until the pork is very tender.
3 Meanwhile, pull the cabbage leaves from the base of the stalk and shred them coarsely. Heat the remaining oil in a pan, add the onion and garlic and cook for a further 3–4 minutes, then add the cabbage and water. Cover, lower the heat and cook gently for 30–40 minutes.
4 When the pork is cooked, remove from the oven and strain any juices remaining in the tin into a small pan. Boil to reduce the juices to about 1 tablespoon, or until they coat the back of a spoon.
5 To serve, put the pork pieces onto serving plates (on a bed of mashed potato, ideally) with the reduced juices drizzled over. Add the cabbage to each serving. Spoon over the salsa verde and serve.

CARBONARA SAUCE

One of the great Italian sauces, rich and extremely unctuous in flavour, carbonara does not traditionally contain any cream. Many cooks, however, feel that the addition of a little cream helps to stabilise the sauce. Although it is generally felt Parmesan is the preferred cheese, any Italian will tell you nothing other than pecorino will do!

serves 4

2 tablespoons olive oil
125g salt pork or smoked bacon, cut into very small dice
1 garlic clove, crushed
3 free-range eggs, lightly beaten
2 tablespoons double cream (optional)
450g dried pasta
50g pecorino (or Reggiano Parmesan) cheese, finely grated
salt and freshly cracked black pepper

1 Heat the oil in a pan, add the pork or bacon and cook until golden all over. Add the garlic and cook for 1 minute.

2 In a bowl, mix the eggs with the cream, if using.

3 Meanwhile, cook the pasta until just done, or *al dente*. Drain well, then add to the bacon and garlic pan. Pour over the eggs, or eggs and cream, quickly add the pecorino and toss to mix. Add salt and pepper to taste and serve immediately.

Variation

FUNGHI CARBONARA

Replace the bacon with 150g fresh, wild mushrooms (or 15g dried and soaked). Proceed as for the main recipe.

PG tip Carbonara is also excellent stirred into scrambled eggs and served on thick, crisp toast.

RAGÙ BOLOGNESE

Although I have not included many sauces cooked with meat or fish as part of the sauce, I felt I had to include this one, because it is so popular. Bolognese sauce as a name doesn't actually exist in Italy, where it is just called a ragù sauce. Tradition has it that the longer the sauce cooks, the better the flavour.

serves 4–6, with pasta

50g unsalted butter
75g pancetta or smoked bacon, cut into small dice
1 onion, finely chopped
1 carrot, finely chopped
1 stick of celery, finely chopped
2 teaspoons chopped oregano
2 teaspoons thyme leaves
350g good-quality lean minced beef
100g chicken livers, cleaned well and chopped
2 tablespoons tomato purée
100ml dry white wine
300ml beef stock **(see page 9)**
salt and freshly cracked black pepper
freshly grated nutmeg

1 Melt the butter in a large, heavy-based pan, add the pancetta and fry for 4–5 minutes, or until golden.

2 Add the onion, carrot, celery and herbs and cook for a further 2 minutes.

3 Stir in the minced beef, increase the heat and brown the meat well all over.

4 Add the chopped livers and cook for 2 minutes. Stir in the tomato purée and cook for 5 minutes.

5 Add the wine and stock, then season lightly with salt, pepper and nutmeg.

6 Bring to the boil, reduce to a low simmer and cook, covered, for at least 30 minutes.

RAGÙ BOLOGNESE

Classically served with Italian noodles, it is also great spooned over fresh gnocchi.

ALMOND AND CAPER SALSA

I first tasted this sauce while on holiday on the beautiful island of Sardinia, at a small restaurant on the Cala di Volpe. It formed a sort of dressing for an aubergine salad, and was wonderful. I have recreated the combination here.

In essence, it is similar to pesto in texture but with added acidic qualities from the capers – a balance of flavours that really works.

makes 250ml

75g blanched almonds, lightly toasted
25g superfine capers, drained and rinsed
a pinch of dried chilli flakes
100ml extra virgin olive oil
1 garlic clove, crushed
25g mint leaves
juice of 1 small lemon
salt

1 Put the almonds, capers and chilli flakes in a blender and blitz to a coarse purée.
2 Heat the oil with the garlic in a pan until warm, then add the mint. Cook for 30 seconds over a very low heat, just to let the flavours infuse.
3 Remove from the heat and leave to cool. Pour in a thin stream through the feeder tube, with the motor running, into the almond and olive mixture in the blender.
4 Add the lemon juice and salt to taste, then transfer the salsa to a bowl and leave to cool completely before serving.

ROASTED AUBERGINE AND TOMATO SALAD WITH ALMOND AND CAPER SALSA

serves 4

2 large aubergines, cut into 2.5cm cubes
2 tablespoons olive oil
1 garlic clove, sliced
2 ripe, firm tomatoes, chopped
1 small onion, chopped
2 tablespoons red wine vinegar
salt and freshly cracked black pepper
2 tablespoons small mint leaves, to garnish
3 tablespoons almond and caper salsa (see left)

1 Preheat the oven to 180°C/350°F/gas mark 4. Place the aubergine cubes in a large roasting tin, drizzle over the oil and toss to coat.
2 Add the garlic, toss again, then roast in the oven until tender, about 20–25 minutes. Turn the aubergine occasionally as it cooks.
3 Transfer to a bowl and leave to cool. Add the tomatoes, onion and vinegar and season to taste.
4 Scatter with the mint leaves and serve with the almond and caper salsa.

PG tip
In some parts of Italy they like to roast the garlic for this recipe, giving the sauce a sweeter, more caramelised flavour.

AGLIATA

An Italian sauce made from pounded walnuts, particularly good with pasta and fish.

makes 200ml

2 slices of stale white bread, crusts removed
60ml chicken stock (see page 9)
1 tablespoon balsamic or red wine vinegar
75g walnut halves, lightly toasted
50g flat-leaf parsley, leaves only
2 garlic cloves, crushed
salt and freshly cracked black pepper
90ml extra virgin olive oil

1 Soak the bread in the stock for 2–3 minutes, then squeeze out the excess moisture, using your hands.
2 Put the bread in a blender with the vinegar, walnuts, parsley, garlic and some salt and pepper.
3 Using the feeder tube and with the motor running, slowly pour in the olive oil until you have a thickish paste-like sauce.
4 Adjust the seasoning and serve. Agliata will keep, covered, in the fridge for 1 day.

LINGUINE WITH RED MULLET AND AGLIATA (for 4 people)

Season 450g small, cleaned red mullet fillets and fry in a mixture of olive oil and unsalted butter for 1 minute on each side. Squeeze over some lemon juice. Meanwhile, cook 450g linguine in boiling, salted water until cooked, then drain and toss with 200ml agliata sauce. Serve with the fried mullet pieces.

SALMORIGLIO

What I adore about this Sicilian garlic, lemon and herb-oil sauce is the way so few ingredients can make something taste so good with fish. I have adapted this recipe from one I tasted on the beautiful island of Sicily. ⊕ *Drizzle it over char-grilled fish and poultry, or use it as a marinade for fish or shellfish.*

makes 150ml

90ml extra virgin olive oil (preferably Sicilian)
1 garlic clove, crushed
2 tablespoons warm water
2 tablespoons chopped oregano
1 tablespoon chopped flat-leaf parsley
juice of ½ lemon
salt and freshly cracked black pepper

1 Whisk the olive oil and garlic together in a bowl, then add the water and whisk to form a light emulsion.

2 Add the herbs and lemon juice and season to taste.

CHAR-GRILLED MONKFISH WITH CHICKPEAS, CHARD AND SALMORIGLIO

serves 4

2 tablespoons olive oil
½ garlic clove, chopped
2 shallots, finely chopped
a pinch of dried chilli flakes
200g tinned tomatoes
1 tablespoon tomato purée
a pinch of sugar
1 small bay leaf
salt and freshly cracked black pepper
400g cooked dried chickpeas (or tinned)
150g Swiss chard leaves, shredded
700g cleaned monkfish fillet, cut into 4 thick pieces
150ml salmoriglio (see left)

1 Heat 1 tablespoon of the oil in a flameproof casserole or pan over a moderate heat. Add the garlic, shallots and chilli flakes and cook for 4–5 minutes, without browning.

2 Add the tomatoes, tomato purée, sugar and bay leaf. Season, then bring to the boil and simmer for 10 minutes.

3 Add the chickpeas and chard, mix well and cook over a low heat for a further 5 minutes.

4 Meanwhile, heat a barbecue or grill pan until very hot. Season the monkfish pieces liberally with salt and pepper and drizzle over the remaining oil.

5 Place the monkfish on the barbecue or grill pan and cook for 4 minutes on each side, until golden and lightly charred.

6 Put the chickpeas on a serving dish, top with the monkfish, drizzle over the salmoriglio sauce and serve.

SICILIAN TOMATO SAUCE

This rustic tomato sauce forms the base of many dishes in Italian cuisine, from pizza to pasta dishes. Ideally, use San Marzano tomatoes for this sauce, as they have a wonderful, sweet flavour. If your tomatoes are not well-flavoured or of a good colour, use tinned.

makes 1 litre

1kg flavourful, ripe tomatoes or 2 x 400g tins plum tomatoes
50ml olive oil
1 large onion, finely chopped
2 garlic cloves, crushed
1 tablespoon tomato purée
150ml tomato juice
a pinch of sugar
½ teaspoon dried oregano
¼ teaspoon thyme leaves
salt and freshly cracked black pepper

1 If using fresh tomatoes, blanch them in boiling water for 20 seconds, then remove them with a slotted spoon directly into iced water. Peel and halve them, then deseed and chop finely.
2 Heat the oil in a heavy-based pan, add the onion and garlic and cook until soft, about 10 minutes.
3 Add the chopped tomatoes and tomato purée and cook for 5 minutes.
4 Add the tomato juice, sugar and herbs and simmer, uncovered, for 1 hour over a low heat, until reduced to a pulpy consistency. Season to taste.

Variations

ARRABIATA SAUCE

Add 2 teaspoons chopped red chilli to the onion and garlic at the beginning of the recipe.

AMATRICIANA SAUCE

Cook 100g chopped pancetta or bacon in the oil until golden, before adding the onion and garlic.

PIRI PIRI

The burning question: is piri piri a sauce or a condiment? In Brazil it brightens up every dish, it seems, so this sauce also has a rightful place in the New World section of this book. However, in Portugal, where I am sure many people first taste it and where it accompanies countless chicken and fish dishes, it is every bit as ubiquitous and popular.

Piri piri sauce, so called after the chilli of the same name, is enjoyed in lots of Mediterranean countries served straight from a bottle: perfectly acceptable, you may say, but in no shape or form a match for the freshly made, preservative-free version here. It will keep for up to a month in the fridge.

makes 350ml

8 large red piri piri or jalapeño chillies
100ml olive oil
200ml tomato passata
1 teaspoon oregano
juice of 1 lemon
a pinch of chilli powder
salt and freshly cracked black pepper

1 Put the chillies and oil in a blender and blitz to a smooth paste.
2 Transfer to a pan and add the passata, oregano and lemon juice. Bring to the boil, then simmer for 10–15 minutes.
3 Add the chilli powder with salt and pepper to taste.

ROMESCU

One of the great Spanish sauces, dating back hundreds of years to Tarragona in the Catalonia region. Whether made with hazelnuts or almonds, it never fails to impress. ⊕ *I think I've served it with just about every type of grilled fish, vegetable, meat, even fried eggs – utterly versatile.*

makes 350ml

150ml extra virgin olive oil
1 slice of white bread, cut into cubes
3 garlic cloves, crushed
75g almonds or hazelnuts, lightly toasted
1 teaspoon dried chilli flakes (or 1 dried red chilli)
1 teaspoon smoked Spanish paprika
350g roasted red peppers
3 tablespoons white wine vinegar
250g tomatoes, blanched, peeled, deseeded and chopped (see Sicilian tomato sauce, page 87, step 1)
salt and freshly cracked black pepper

1 Heat 25ml of the oil in a large frying pan, add the bread cubes and fry until golden. Add the garlic, almonds or hazelnuts, chilli flakes and paprika, and cook for a further 30 seconds.

2 Transfer to a blender and add the roasted peppers and vinegar. Blitz to a pulp. Using the feeder tube and with the motor running, gradually trickle in the remaining olive oil.

3 Add the tomatoes, blitz again and season to taste.

Variation

SPICY ROMESCU VINAGRETTE

Add 2 tablespoons of the romescu sauce to 150ml classic vinaigrette (see page 62). Great with grilled tuna or swordfish.

ROASTED SWORDFISH WITH FENNEL, PINE NUTS AND RAISINS

serves 4

75g olive oil
1 onion, thinly sliced
1 head of fennel, thinly sliced, fronds reserved and chopped
a pinch of sugar
50g pine nuts, lightly toasted
50g raisins, soaked in water for 20 minutes and drained
4 swordfish steaks, 200g each
salt and freshly cracked black pepper
2 tablespoons chopped mint leaves
100ml romescu sauce (see left)

1 Heat 50ml of the oil in a pan, add the onion, fennel and sugar and cook over a low heat until lightly caramelised and golden.

2 Add the pine nuts and drained raisins and cook for a further 5 minutes.

3 Meanwhile, heat the remaining oil in a frying pan and season the fish. When the oil is hot, add the fish and cook for 1–2 minutes on each side until golden. Put the swordfish and fennel mixture on a plate.

4 Add the chopped mint and fennel fronds to the romescu sauce and serve alongside the swordfish.

AVGOLEMONO

One of the most popular and ubiquitous sauces in Greece, this lemon sauce is delicious served with meat and vegetables such as artichokes, leeks or asparagus. ⊕ *I particularly like it with foil-baked cod steaks on a melée of butter beans, tomato and parsley, as in the recipe on the right.*

makes 400ml

3 large free-range egg yolks
juice of 2 lemons
2 teaspoons cornflour
1 tablespoon water
300ml well-flavoured hot chicken stock (see page 8)
2 tablespoons sour cream
salt and freshly cracked black pepper

1 Whisk the egg yolks and lemon juice together in a heavy-based pan, off the heat.

2 Put the cornflour and water in a jar with a lid and shake until dissolved. Stir it into the egg yolks in the pan.

3 Whisk the hot stock gradually into the eggs, a little at a time, until amalgamated, whisking constantly, then add the cream.

4 Place the pan over a low heat and cook, whisking continuously, until the mixture thickens enough to coat the back of a spoon. Make sure that it does not boil, or the sauce will curdle.

5 Season to taste and serve immediately.

PG tip Avgolemono is also the name of a soup made in Greece, of chicken broth with rice, finished with egg and lemon.

BAKED COD STEAKS WITH BUTTER BEANS AND AVGOLEMONO

The cod here can be substituted for halibut, if you like.

serves 4

1 small onion, chopped
2 rashers of streaky bacon, chopped
1 tablespoon olive oil
1 garlic clove, crushed
¼ teaspoon dried chilli flakes
100g dried butter beans
800ml well-flavoured hot chicken stock (see page 8)
3 plum tomatoes, roughly chopped
1 tablespoon chopped flat-leaf parsley
salt and freshly cracked black pepper
4 cod steaks, 225g each
2 shallots, thinly sliced
juice of ½ lemon
150ml fish stock (see page 9)
150ml avgolemono (see left), to serve

1 Preheat the oven to 160°C/325°F/gas mark 3. In a large ovenproof casserole, sweat the onion and bacon in the oil over a low heat for 3–4 minutes. Add the garlic, chilli flakes and butter beans and cook for 1 minute.

2 Pour on the chicken stock, bring to the boil, cover and cook for 2 hours until the beans are very tender, adding a little extra stock or water if needed.

3 Stir in the tomatoes and parsley, season to taste and remove from the heat.

4 Increase the oven temperature to 220°C/425°F/gas mark 7. Place the fish steaks in a baking tin and scatter with the shallots. Add the lemon juice and fish stock, then season. Cover with foil and cook in the oven for 10–12 minutes, or until the fish is cooked through.

5 Divide the beans between 4 individual plates, top each with a baked cod steak, pour over the hot avgolemono sauce and serve immediately.

SKORDALIA

Skordalia (or as it is known throughout Greece, Skorthalia) is a delightful sauce of just four components: potatoes, olive oil, garlic and lemon juice – magically simple. It works better when the potatoes are still warm, so don't let them go cold. In certain parts of Greece, chopped walnuts are added to the potatoes before blending. ⊕ *A great sauce for almost any fish, especially deep-fried. It also makes a useful dip at parties for vegetables or pitta bread.*

makes 750ml

300g floury potatoes (e.g. Maris Piper or Desirée), cut into chunks
4 garlic cloves, crushed
175–200ml extra virgin olive oil
juice of ½ large lemon
salt and freshly cracked black pepper

1 Put the potatoes in a pan of cold water, bring to the boil and simmer for 20–25 minutes until very soft. Drain well, then transfer to a food processor or blender.
2 Add the garlic and blitz quickly. With the motor running on its slowest possible setting, pour in enough oil in a thin stream to form an emulsion.
3 Add the lemon juice and enough warm water to achieve a mayonnaise-like consistency.
4 Season to taste and serve.

Variation

Add 75g feta cheese to the hot potatoes in the blender, then proceed as for the main recipe.

PG tip Don't work the potatoes too long in the blender or processor, as they will turn starchy and glutinous.

ROASTED BEETS WITH ROCKET, SOFT EGG AND SKORDALIA

serves 4

24 baby raw beetroots (or 2–3 larger beetroots, sliced)
2 tablespoons olive oil
salt and freshly cracked black pepper
4 free-range eggs
350ml skordalia (see left)
100g baby rocket leaves
25g coriander leaves (optional)
2 tablespoons classic vinaigrette (see page 62)

1 Preheat the oven to 200°C/400°F/gas mark 6. Trim the beetroots, leaving about 2.5cm of long top attached. Trim the bottoms to remove any root.
2 Toss the beetroots in the olive oil and season with a little salt. Put them in a baking dish, cover with foil and cook in the oven for up to 45 minutes, or until tender when pierced with a knife.
3 Remove from the oven and leave until cool enough to handle, then peel. Season with salt and pepper and keep warm.
4 Cook the eggs in simmering water for 5 minutes so that the yolks are still soft in the middle. Remove, cool and peel.
5 To serve, place some skordalia on the base of 4 serving plates, with the beetroots on top. Scatter over the rocket (and coriander if using) and drizzle the vinaigrette on top. Halve the eggs and add to each plate, then serve immediately.

TARATOR

This sauce is one of Turkey's greatest treasures. It is traditionally made with hazelnuts, although local cooks tend to make it with whatever nuts grow locally in their area. I prefer to use almonds, although all nuts generally work well. ⊕ *Great with grilled and deep-fried foods.*

makes 300ml

3 thick slices of white bread, crusts removed
100ml full-fat milk
150g almonds (or any other good-quality nuts)
3 garlic cloves, crushed
120ml olive oil
salt and freshly cracked black pepper
juice of 1 lemon

1 Put the bread in a bowl, cover with the milk and leave to soak for 30 minutes.
2 Transfer to a blender, add the almonds and garlic and blitz to a paste.
3 Using the feeder tube, pour in the oil in a thin stream with the motor running, to form an emulsion. Season and add lemon juice to taste.

TAHINI SAUCE

⊕ *This famous Middle Eastern sauce is great not only as a dip to serve with falafel, but also as a wonderful dressing for my bean, mint and chickpea salad (see below).*

makes 300ml

150g tahini (sesame seed paste)
3 garlic cloves, crushed
juice of 1 lemon
1 teaspoon ground cumin
a pinch each of cayenne pepper, ground coriander and ground cardamom
75–120ml hot water
salt

1 Put the tahini and garlic in a blender and add the lemon juice and spices.
2 Slowly add the hot water through the feeder tube, with the motor running, until the sauce has a dropping consistency. Season and transfer to a bowl.

Variations

Finish the sauce with 50ml thick, natural yoghurt and 2 tablespoons chopped mint: fantastic with grilled aubergine slices.

Add some zip with a little chopped red chilli or Tabasco sauce.

GREEN BEAN, MINT AND CHICKPEA SALAD (for 4 people)

Put 300g cooked green beans and 400g tinned or cooked dried chickpeas in a bowl with a handful of mint leaves. Add salt, pepper and lemon juice to taste. Stir in 4 tablespoons tahini sauce and mix well. Sprinkle some more mint leaves on top and serve at room temperature.

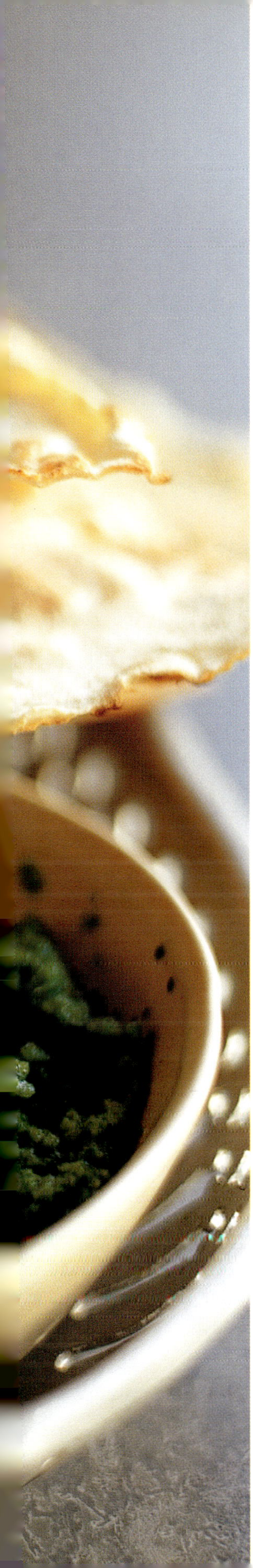

ZHOUG

A hot and extremely fragrant chilli-pepper sauce from the Yemen. ⊕ *Wonderful with meat, fish and poultry; I also like to add it to vegetable broths. It is sometimes made with red chilli, but I prefer the flavour of green here.*

makes 300ml

10 green jalapeño chillies, deseeded
4 garlic cloves, crushed
a good bunch of flat-leaf parsley
a good bunch of coriander leaves
1 teaspoon ground cumin
½ teaspoon ground coriander
a pinch of cayenne pepper
100ml olive oil
salt and freshly cracked black pepper

1 Put the chillies and garlic in a blender and blitz until smooth.

2 Add the herbs, spices and enough water to blitz into a smooth paste.

3 Add the olive oil, season to taste and blitz for a final minute.

4 Transfer the sauce to a bowl, cover and refrigerate until ready to use. It will keep in the fridge for up to 3 months.

PG tip Shatta, another Middle Eastern hot sauce, is prepared in the same way, but with milder, red chillies, which results in a slightly milder flavour. Great for giving a salad dressing a lift.

HARISSA

This spiced red chilli sauce is found throughout the Maghreb, especially in Tunisia and Morocco. In Algeria it is also known as dersa. It is served alongside almost everything savoury – from tagines to grilled fish, or just simply as a dip in which to immerse chunks of crusty bread. Although there are some good varieties of pre-made harissa now available, there are as many that are poorly made, so it's always better to make your own. It lasts for up to 1 month in the fridge, or 3 months in the freezer.

makes 350ml

5 red jalapeño chillies, roughly chopped
200g tinned plum tomatoes
3 garlic cloves, crushed
1 tablespoon tomato purée
1 tablespoon ground cumin
2 teaspoons hot curry powder
1 teaspoon ground caraway
1 teaspoon ground coriander
½ teaspoon cayenne pepper
50ml olive oil
a dash of vinegar
a pinch of coarse salt

1 Put all the ingredients except the vinegar and salt in a blender and blitz to a smooth, thickish paste.
2 Transfer to a bowl and add the vinegar and salt.

LAMB AND MERGUEZ BROCHETTES WITH SQUASH AND MINT COUS COUS

In this tasty lamb dish the harissa is used as a marinade for the meat. For those who enjoy the adrenaline pleasures of hot food, serve a little harissa with the dish as well.

serves 4

4 trimmed lamb chumps, 200g each, cut into large cubes
175g merguez sausages, thickly sliced
2 tablespoons harissa (see left)
juice of ½ lemon
1 tablespoon olive oil

for the cous cous

400g peeled butternut squash, cut into cubes
200g cous cous
200ml hot chicken stock (see page 9)
4 tablespoons chopped mint leaves
2 tablespoons olive oil
a pinch of ground cumin
salt and freshly cracked black pepper
saffron-infused natural yoghurt, to serve

1 Put the lamb and merguez in a bowl and add the harissa, lemon juice, oil and some salt. Leave, covered, at room temperature for 1 hour.
2 Thread alternate cubes of lamb and merguez on to 4 pre-soaked wooden skewers, then set aside.
3 Preheat a barbecue or grill pan and cook for 6–8 minutes until the meat is charred all over but pink in the middle, turning regularly as it cooks.
4 Meanwhile, cook the squash on the barbecue or in the grill pan until lightly charred and tender.
5 Put the cous cous in a bowl and add the hot stock, then cover with clingfilm and leave to stand for 2–3 minutes. Remove the clingfilm and fluff up the grains with a fork. Add the grilled squash, mint, oil, cumin and salt and pepper to taste.
6 Serve the meat on top of the cous cous, with the saffron yoghurt.

MESHWIYA

Tunisia's answer to the Mexican salsa, hot and heady, but at the same time fresh and lively.

⊕ *Serve it with a spice-roasted leg of lamb or grilled lamb chops, but on a hot summer's day spread it on thick slices of baguette while the barbecue is heating up!*

makes 150ml

3 ripe but firm plum tomatoes, chopped into small pieces
1 large red pepper, roasted, deseeded and chopped into small pieces
1 teaspoon harissa (see page 98)
2 garlic cloves, crushed
1 teaspoon ground cumin
2 tablespoons olive oil
juice of ½ lemon
2 tablespoons chopped flat-leaf parsley
salt and freshly cracked black pepper

1 Heat a dry frying pan over a medium heat, then add the tomatoes and red pepper and cook for 1 minute, or until the tomatoes are just beginning to soften. Add the harissa and cook for a further 1 minute.

2 Transfer to a bowl and add the remaining ingredients. Mix well, season to taste and serve at room temperature.

THE AMERICAS

There is a saying, 'Taste a country's cuisine and you will taste its culture.' Nowhere is this more apparent than in the countries of South America and the Caribbean. There, they reject the traditional, dairy-based sauces of France and Europe in favour of light, piquant salsas and relishes, highly flavoured with chillies, limes, herbs and spices. These ingredients not only add taste, texture and colour but also make a bold and exciting statement. They stimulate the eye while enlivening the palate. Furthermore, they are simple to prepare and extremely healthy.

It's almost impossible to imagine a meal without sauces in the Americas. In Mexico, breakfast eggs are invariably accompanied by a bowl of salsa fresca, an uncooked tomato relish, while in the evening more complex sauces, made of toasted and ground dried chillies and spices, are enjoyed. In the Caribbean, there are the Creole sauces popular in the French-speaking islands, or the soffrito of Spanish-speaking islands such as Cuba. Sauces like these are also found in the Deep South of the United States, which has strong historical links with the Caribbean.

CREOLE SAUCE

A classic most Creole locals know as 'red gravy', this is the basis for the famous shrimp Creole or any fish dish that calls for a lightly spiced red sauce. Like many sauces from this region, it begins with a little 'holy trinity' of sautéed onion, celery and sweet pepper. ⊕ *It works well with any firm fish such as snapper or monkfish.*

makes 750ml

25g unsalted butter
1 tablespoon olive oil
1 onion, chopped
2 sticks of celery, thinly sliced
2 garlic cloves, crushed
1 green pepper, deseeded and cut into 2cm dice
½ teaspoon ground cumin
½ teaspoon oregano leaves
1 tablespoon tomato purée
1 teaspoon white wine vinegar
300ml chicken stock (see page 9)
60ml dry white wine
1 teaspoon Worcestershire sauce
2 tablespoons chopped flat-leaf parsley
1 bay leaf
salt and a pinch of chilli powder

1 Heat the butter and oil in a pan, then add the onion, celery, garlic and green pepper. Cook over a low heat until softened and with just a little colour.

2 Add the cumin and oregano and cook for a further 1 minute.

3 Stir in the tomato purée and cook for a further 2 minutes.

4 Add the vinegar, stock, wine, Worcestershire sauce, parsley and bay leaf. Mix well, then cook for 2–3 minutes. Season with salt and chilli powder.

CREOLE SNAPPER WITH CRISPY SPICY ONIONS

serves 4

4 snapper fillets, 175g each, cut in half lengthways
juice of 2 limes
1 garlic clove, crushed
salt and freshly cracked black pepper
2 tablespoons olive oil
250 ml creole sauce (see left)

for the onions

1 tablespoon Cajun spices
1 tablespoon plain flour
2 onions, thinly sliced and separated into rings
2 tablespoons full-fat milk
oil, for deep-frying
flat-leaf parsley, to serve

1 Place the fish in a non-reactive dish, toss gently with the lime juice, garlic and some salt and pepper and leave to marinate for 30 minutes. Remove and dry on kitchen paper.

2 Heat the oil in a frying pan and, when it is hot, add the fish and fry for 1–2 minutes on each side, until golden. Remove to a plate. Add the creole sauce to the pan, top with the fish, cover and lightly braise for 4–5 minutes.

3 Meanwhile, to make the crispy onions, mix the Cajun spices and flour together in a bowl. Dip the onions into the milk, then into the flour and spice mixture, shaking off any excess.

4 Deep-fry in hot oil (165°C/325°F) until crisp and golden, then drain on kitchen paper.

5 Spoon the fish and sauce onto a serving dish, top with the spicy onions and serve garnished with flat-leaf parsley.

MEXICAN SALSA VERDE

The following two sauces, green and red, are perhaps the staple of the Mexican kitchen: one or the other seems to accompany almost every meal. Salsa verde can be made either roasted or raw; it's down to personal taste, so I am giving my favourite, the roasted version.

Salsa roja is traditionally roasted and therefore tends to be the more heady of the two. Both versions are poured over meat, fish or egg dishes.

You can use a mortar and pestle rather than a blender for the first two steps of this recipe if you prefer.

PG tip – a note on chillies
Serrano chillies are sold red or mature green, moderate to very hot, with an intense bite. They are often used in Thai cooking, but are more synonymous with Mexico and the southwestern United States. Jalapeño (pronounced halapenyo) chillies are green when matured, hot with an immediate bite. They are sold fresh, canned or pickled.

Both serrano and jalapeño chillies can be bought from spice shops and some good supermarkets. If they are unavailable, any good hot green chilli will be fine.

makes 200ml

2 green serrano chillies
1 green jalapeño chilli
6 fresh tomatillos or small green tomatoes, halved
1 small onion, chopped
2 garlic cloves, crushed
a few small handfuls of coriander leaves
salt and a good pinch of ground cumin

1 In a dry frying pan, toast the chillies, stirring for 1 minute until aromatic and lightly charred with darkened spots. Transfer to a blender.
2 Add the tomatillos to the same dry pan and fry until charred, then add to the blender.
3 Add the onion, garlic and coriander to the blender. Blitz with enough water to form a sauce-like consistency.
4 Season with salt and cumin.The salsa will keep well for several days in the fridge.

SALSA ROJA

The endless varieties of chilli in Mexico bring different qualities to food: the nuttiness of cascabel, the searing heat of de árbol and the smokiness of the red chipotle variety, but any dried chilli will give you the required punch. This sauce is also often known as enchilada sauce.

makes 200ml

10g small, hot, dried chillies (de árbol or ancho)
4 garlic cloves, unpeeled
4 ripe but firm plum tomatoes, halved
½ teaspoon sugar
½ teaspoon dried oregano
1 tablespoon vegetable oil
a good pinch of ground cumin
salt

1 In a dry frying pan, toast the chillies, stirring for 1 minute until they become aromatic and lightly charred with darkened spots. Transfer to a bowl, cover with hot water and leave to soak for 30 minutes.

2 In the same pan, toast the garlic, turning often, until softened and darkened in places, about 15 minutes. Leave to cool, then peel.

3 Add the tomatoes to the same pan and dry-fry over a low heat until charred, about 5 minutes each side. Transfer to a blender.

4 Drain the soaked chillies and add to the tomatoes in the blender. Blitz, adding enough water to give a sauce-like consistency.

5 Add the sugar, oregano, oil, cumin and a little salt, then blitz for a further 30 seconds. The salsa will keep well for several days in the fridge.

SALSA FRESCA

(or salsa cruda)

The simplest of table sauces in Mexican cuisine; every family has their own particular favourite. It is fresh-tasting and extremely moreish. Salsas are a great time-saver in the kitchen: incredibly easy to make, and perfect with eggs, beans, tortilla chips, shellfish and poultry dishes. For utmost freshness, don't make them too far in advance, and use them as soon as possible after they have infused. The red chillies can be replaced with green or yellow varieties.

makes 200ml

300g ripe but firm vine tomatoes, cut into small dice
1 red onion, cut into small dice
2 red jalapeño chillies, finely chopped
1 tablespoon caster sugar or maple syrup
juice of 3 limes
2 garlic cloves, crushed
2 tablespoons each chopped oregano and coriander

1 Mix all the ingredients together in a bowl and leave to infuse for at least 30 minutes before using.

Variations

In certain parts of Mexico, spices such as ground cumin or cayenne pepper, and herbs such as oregano are added to the salsas; variations are limitless, so add whatever herb or spice you feel will work well.

PICO DE GALLO

Literally translating as 'rooster's beak', this is a similar, but hotter, Mexican table sauce, using the same recipe but with the chillies char-grilled before being chopped and with 2 tablespoons distilled white vinegar instead of the lime juice.

MEXICAN SALSA VERDE

Tomatillos are unfortunately not always easy to find; green tomatoes are an acceptable substitute, but they do not have the apple-and-lemon tartness of tomatillos.

PG tip

Limes can sometimes be a bit hard and the juice difficult to extract. In this case, simply place in a microwave for 10 seconds (no longer or the juice will get very hot) to loosen the juices from within.

CHIMOL

This is a fresh, simple and tasty sauce from El Salvador. ⊕ *I love it with cumin-rubbed flank steak cooked on the barbecue, and also spooned over marinated goat's cheese crushed on to tortilla chips.*

makes 200ml

4 vine tomatoes, halved
2 tablespoons olive oil
a good bunch of coriander
juice of 2 limes
3 tablespoons chopped mint leaves
1 small red onion, finely chopped
4 red radishes, finely chopped
½ teaspoon ground cumin
a pinch of dried chilli flakes
salt

1 Heat a grill pan until hot. Brush the tomato halves with the olive oil and cook on the grill pan until lightly charred and softened.
2 Meanwhile, combine all the remaining ingredients in a bowl, with salt to taste.
3 Mash the grilled tomatoes into the bowl and mix thoroughly. Adjust the seasoning and leave to stand for 30 minutes, to infuse, before serving.

AJILIMOJILI

A hot garlic, pepper and chilli sauce from Puerto Rico. ⊕ *Excellent served with roast pork or used as a marinade for meat and fish.*

makes 300ml

3 hot red chillies (preferably serrano), deseeded and chopped
2 red peppers, halved, deseeded and roughly chopped
4 black peppercorns
4 garlic cloves
salt
juice of 4 limes
100ml olive oil
3 tablespoons chopped coriander

1 Put the chillies and red peppers in a mortar (or blender) with the peppercorns, garlic and some salt and pound (or blitz) to a paste.
2 Add the lime juice and oil and work (or blitz) to a purée. The finished sauce will keep for up to 1 week in a sealed container in the fridge.

MEXICAN RED MOLE

Mole (pronounced mo-lay), from the Spanish word for to grind, is Mexico's national dish, which may surprise you if your experience of Mexican cooking extends no further than enchiladas or burritos. Every Mexican home has its favourite mole recipe, and there are countless versions. They always contain ground seeds or nuts and, of course, chillies, and are usually served with chicken or meat. This red mole offers a sauce of sweetness, a little bitterness, nuttiness and earthiness all at once, if you can imagine it.

Don't be put off by the long ingredients list; mole is worth the time it takes to make. Crisp corn tortillas are available from specialist shops; do not use flour tortillas, as they are completely different.

makes 1 litre

2 dried ancho chillies
2 dried pasilla chillies or ½ teaspoon dried chilli flakes
750ml chicken stock (see page 9)
2 corn tortillas, 15cm diameter
1 tablespoon lard or vegetable oil
1 onion, chopped
½ teaspoon dried oregano
2 garlic cloves, crushed
400g tinned tomatoes
50g raisins, soaked in water until plump, then drained
75g dark unsweetened Mexican chocolate (see tip, right)
2 tablespoons peanut butter
1 tablespoon white wine vinegar
1 teaspoon sugar
½ teaspoon ground cinnamon
½ teaspoon ground cloves
1 teaspoon coriander seeds
1 tablespoon sesame seeds, toasted
a pinch of ground aniseed
salt

1 Heat a dry frying pan, then add the chillies and dry-fry until fragrant and charred in places. Transfer to a bowl, cover with water and leave to soak for 30 minutes.

2 Pour 250ml of the chicken stock into a pan and bring to the boil. Add the tortillas, then remove from the heat.

3 Heat half the lard or oil in a separate pan and add the onion, oregano and garlic. Cook for 3–4 minutes until softened.

4 Remove the chillies from the water and roughly chop. Add to the onions in the pan and cook for 30 seconds.

5 Pour in the tortilla-infused stock (the tortillas will have dissolved into the stock by now) and bring to the boil.

6 Add the tomatoes and the rest of the ingredients except for the stock, with a little salt, then transfer the mixture to a blender and blitz until smooth.

7 Return to the pan, add the remaining stock and simmer for 12–15 minutes.

SIMPLE RED MOLE CHICKEN

Sear some chicken pieces in a flameproof casserole until golden all over. Pour the red mole sauce over the chicken, cover with a lid or foil and bake in the oven at 190°C/375°F/gas mark 5 for 45 minutes or until the chicken is cooked. Sprinkle with a few toasted sesame seeds before serving.

PG tip Mexican chocolate differs from the sort commonly found in Europe; some types are very sweet while others have no sweetening at all. It is often flavoured, with some brands containing cinnamon. If you are travelling in Mexico, look out for chocolate from Oaxaca or Puebla, and bring some home! Otherwise, just use chocolate with the highest possible percentage of cocoa solids – at least 70 per cent.

MOJO CRIOLLO

Mojo is the collective name of several hot sauces and relishes which originated in the Canary Islands. Basically consisting of olive oil, garlic, chilli and cumin with an acid component such as vinegar or lemon, they are served at the beginning of a meal.

Somewhat similar-style mojos can be found in the Caribbean and in Cuba, where they are the national table sauce – mojo is to Cuban cuisine what salsa is to Mexican and vinaigrettes are to French. This recipe is for perhaps the most famous of all mojos. ⊕ *Serve with just about anything; grilled fish and meat are especially good. Mojos taste best when served a couple of hours after they are made.*

makes 300ml

75ml olive oil
2 garlic cloves, crushed
125ml sour (Seville) orange juice or half-and-half lime juice and orange juice
1 teaspoon cumin seeds
1 hot red chilli, deseeded and finely chopped
1 teaspoon sherry vinegar (optional)
1 tablespoon tomato ketchup (optional)
salt and freshly cracked black pepper

1 Put the oil and garlic in a pan and heat gently until lightly golden but not browned, about 30 seconds.
2 Add the orange juice or lime and orange juice mix, the cumin and chilli, bring to the boil and simmer for 3–4 minutes until slightly reduced.
3 Remove from the heat and leave to cool slightly before adding the vinegar and ketchup, if using. Season to taste and leave to infuse for a couple of hours before serving. Mojo will keep, covered, in the fridge for up to 2 days.

Variations

MOJO DE AJO (garlic mojo)

Replace the chilli with pickled red chillies and add double the amount of garlic (4 cloves). When the mixture is cool, add 2 tablespoons chopped flat-leaf parsley.

RED ONION, GRAPEFRUIT AND CORIANDER MOJO

Proceed as for the basic recipe, but replace the orange juice with grapefruit juice and add ½ small chopped red onion and a few chopped coriander leaves at the end before cooling. Ideal with freshly flaked crab meat.

MANGO AND MINT MOJO

Add ½ chopped fresh mango and 2 tablespoons roughly chopped mint leaves to the basic mojo recipe. Fantastic with lamb chops.

PERUVIAN AJÍ SAUCE

A green dipping sauce from Peru, where ají denotes a hot variety of chilli. ⊕ *It is fantastic with small steamed prawns.*

makes 250ml

1 green jalapeño chilli
½ head of Cos lettuce
125ml mayonnaise (see page 30)
2 slices of white bread, crusts removed, soaked in 50ml water
a good handful of coriander leaves

1 Heat a dry frying pan over a moderate heat, add the chilli and dry-fry until charred all over, about 2–3 minutes. Remove and cool.

2 Remove the centre core from the lettuce and cut the remaining leaves into small pieces.

3 Put the lettuce and roasted chillies in a blender with the mayonnaise and blitz to a purée.

4 Squeeze the excess moisture from the bread and add to the blender with the coriander. Blitz to a smooth purée. The finished sauce will keep, covered, for up to 2 days in the fridge.

SALSA DE MANI

⊕ *In Ecuador, this creamy peanut sauce usually accompanies the popular deep-fried potato croquettes. It is also wonderful when used as a base for braised chicken (see below).*

makes 600ml

2 tablespoons olive oil
1 onion, finely chopped
2 garlic cloves, crushed
1 large red pepper, halved, deseeded and cut into strips
1 teaspoon ground cumin
½ teaspoon dried oregano
1 tablespoon tomato purée
400g tinned tomatoes
3 tablespoons smooth peanut butter
salt and freshly cracked black pepper

1 Heat the oil in a pan, add the onion, garlic and red pepper and cook for 3–5 minutes until the vegetables begin to soften.

2 Add the cumin, oregano, tomato purée and tomatoes and bring to the boil. Cook for 8–10 minutes until the sauce becomes flavourful and thickened.

3 Stir in the peanut butter, season to taste and cook for a further 5 minutes. The sauce will keep in the fridge, covered, for 2–3 days.

BRAISED CHICKEN WITH CREAMED PEANUTS AND TOMATOES

(for 4 people)

Joint a 1.5–1.8kg free-range chicken and season with salt and pepper. Fry in 2 tablespoons hot vegetable oil for 5–6 minutes, turning a few times, until golden all over. Add 600ml salsa de mani with 250ml chicken stock (see page 9) and mix well. Cover and simmer for a further 12–15 minutes until the chicken is cooked and tender.

SALSA RANCHERO

Salsa means sauce in Spanish, and in Latin America it is generally an uncooked mixture of chillies and tomatoes. ⊕ *This chunky version has a great affinity with egg dishes, but also with chicken and fish. It is not overly hot and can be enjoyed by those who do not care for sauces that raise your temperature!*

makes 300ml

2 tablespoons vegetable oil
1 onion, finely chopped
3 garlic cloves
1 red jalapeño chilli, chopped
6 ripe but firm tomatoes, chopped (or 200g tinned)
1 teaspoon tomato purée
a pinch of sugar
1 teaspoon ground cumin
1 teaspoon chopped oregano
1 tablespoon chopped coriander

1 Heat the oil in a pan, add the onion, garlic and chilli and cook for 8–10 minutes, until softened.
2 Add the tomatoes, tomato purée, sugar, cumin, oregano and coriander, and simmer over a low heat for 10–12 minutes, for the flavours to infuse.
3 Remove from the heat and leave to cool. The sauce will keep, covered, in the fridge for 2–3 days.

HUEVOS RANCHEROS

I first enjoyed this dish of Mexican ranch-style eggs in Texas, while staying at The Mansion on Turtle Creek about 15 years ago. I was introduced to it by the then chef, good friend and pioneer of Tex-Mex cooking, Dean Fearing. It soon became a favourite of mine: a great breakfast or light brunch option.

serves 4

4 tablespoons vegetable oil
1 small onion, finely chopped
1 garlic clove, crushed
1 red chilli, finely chopped
125g cooked black beans, lightly crushed
½ teaspoon ground cumin
4 corn tortillas
4 free-range eggs
100g guacamole (see tip below)
150ml salsa ranchero (see left), to serve

1 Heat 1 tablespoon of the oil in a pan, add the onion, garlic and chilli and cook for 2 minutes, without browning them. Add the beans and cumin, and cook until heated through. Remove from the heat and keep warm.
2 Heat 1 teaspoon of the oil in a large frying pan and fry each tortilla, one at a time and adding more oil as needed, until crisp and golden. Remove, drain on kitchen paper and keep warm.
3 Add the remaining oil to the pan and fry the eggs.
4 To serve, place a crisp tortilla on each serving plate and top with fried beans. Top each with a fried egg and a good dollop of guacamole. Spoon over the salsa ranchero and serve.

PG tip – guacamole

Cut 1 large avocado in half and remove the stone. Scoop the flesh into a bowl and mash lightly with a fork, leaving a few lumps. Stir in ½ red onion, finely chopped, 1 green chilli, deseeded and finely chopped, 25g chopped coriander, 1 deseeded and finely chopped ripe tomato, 2 tablespoons lime juice and salt to taste. Use immediately, or cover with clingfilm to prevent the avocado turning brown.

SIMPLE CAJUN KETCHUP

Everyone loves ketchup smothered over a burger or crispy fries. You just can't beat it – sweet and toothsome. The addition of a little heat via some Cajun spices adds another flavour dimension.

makes 300ml

1 tablespoon olive oil
1 large onion, finely chopped
8 very ripe, sweet tomatoes, deseeded and roughly chopped
45g soft brown sugar
2 tablespoons black treacle or molasses
3 tablespoons white wine vinegar or cider vinegar
2 tablespoons tomato purée
½ teaspoon mustard powder
1 tablespoon Cajun spices
juice of ½ lemon
salt and freshly cracked black pepper

1 Heat the oil in a pan until very hot. Add the onion and tomatoes, cover and leave over a high heat for 3–4 minutes.
2 Add the remaining ingredients, except the lemon juice and seasoning, lower the heat and cook, uncovered, for 25 minutes, stirring occasionally.
3 Remove from the heat and add the lemon juice. Transfer to a blender and blitz until smooth (for a really smooth ketchup, strain it through a sieve too).
4 Season with salt and pepper, then leave to cool completely before serving. Alternatively, keep in the fridge until needed, for up to 1 month.

PG tip If you can't buy Cajun spices, make your own: in a mortar and pestle, crush to a fairly fine powder 1 teaspoon each of chopped garlic, cayenne pepper, paprika, dried thyme and dried oregano and a little salt and pepper.

PEBRE SAUCE

In Chile, this hot sauce accompanies just about everything. The heat varies from one cook to another, with some versions only mildly hot, and others leading you to seek solace in a cool drink. This recipe is the way I like it: not too hot, but with purpose.

makes 300ml

2 small hot red chillies (or ½ teaspoon Tabasco sauce)
120ml olive oil
1 onion, finely chopped
2 tablespoons chopped coriander
2 tablespoons chopped flat-leaf parsley
3 garlic cloves, crushed
1 teaspoon oregano
4 tablespoons red wine vinegar
salt and freshly cracked black pepper

1 Put the chillies with half the oil in a blender and blitz to a purée. Transfer to a bowl.
2 Add the remaining ingredients and adjust the seasoning to taste. Leave covered for 2 hours at room temperature for the flavours to infuse. The sauce will keep in the fridge, covered, for up to 3 days, but is at its best eaten on the day it is made.

SOFRITO

Sofrito is one of the cornerstones and treasures of Spanish Caribbean cuisine, the smell of sautéed onions, garlic and peppers pervading from homes everywhere. ⊕ *Use as a base for soups, stews and rice dishes, much as for the Italian version, soffrito. It also makes a great topping for pizzas or crostini.*

makes 350ml

2 tablespoons olive oil or melted pork fat
1 onion, finely chopped
3 garlic cloves, crushed
2 red peppers, halved, deseeded and finely diced
½ teaspoon ground cumin
½ teaspoon dried oregano
1 bay leaf
200g tinned tomatoes, finely chopped
salt and freshly cracked black pepper
2 tablespoons chopped coriander

1 Heat the oil in a non-stick frying pan and add the onion, garlic, red peppers, cumin, oregano and bay leaf. Cook over a low heat for 5–6 minutes until softened.
2 Add the tomatoes with some salt and pepper, and cook slowly until reduced and thickened. Stir in the coriander and season with a little extra cumin, if liked. Sofrito will keep, refrigerated, for 3–4 days.

SALSA GUASACACA

⊕ *A colourful Venezuelan variation of guacamole, traditionally served with grilled meats. I also love it with hard-boiled eggs.*

makes 200ml

1 large, ripe avocado (preferably Hass)
4 tablespoons olive oil
1 garlic clove, crushed
2 tablespoons red wine vinegar
½ teaspoon hot red chilli sauce (or 1 hot red chilli, finely chopped)
salt and freshly cracked black pepper
2 vine tomatoes, deseeded and cut into 5mm dice
1 small green pepper, halved, deseeded and finely chopped
1 small red pepper, halved, deseeded and finely chopped
2 free-range eggs, hard-boiled, peeled and chopped
1 tablespoon chopped flat-leaf parsley
1 tablespoon chopped coriander

1 Cut the avocado in half and remove the stone and skin. Mash one half and set aside. Chop the other half into small dice.
2 In a bowl, mix the oil, garlic, vinegar, chilli sauce or chilli and salt and pepper.
3 Add the tomatoes, green and red peppers, eggs, herbs and chopped avocado. Gently mix together.
4 Fold in the mashed avocado, adjust the seasoning to taste and serve.

MINT CHIMICHURRI

Classic chimichurri is the ultimate companion for steak throughout Argentina, though I first tasted it smeared generously over smoked brisket and tucked up in a soft bap roll at a barbecue in Houston, Texas. It certainly made an impression and now regularly appears on my menus. It could be described, I suppose, as Latin America's answer to pesto. Traditionally, only parsley and oregano are used, but here is my favourite variation on the theme, using mint. For the traditional version, omit the mint and use double the quantity of parsley.

⊕ *The minty sauce makes a great marinade for steaks and vegetables.*

makes 300ml

1 bunch of mint leaves
1 small bunch of flat-leaf parsley
1 teaspoon dried chilli flakes
3 garlic cloves, crushed
100ml mild olive oil
4 tablespoons water
3 tablespoons red wine vinegar
1 teaspoon dried oregano
salt and freshly cracked black pepper
4 plum tomatoes, peeled, deseeded and chopped (optional)

1 Put the mint and parsley in a blender, add the chilli flakes and garlic and blitz until fine.
2 Add the oil, water, vinegar, oregano and a little salt and pepper, then blitz until slightly coarse. Add the tomatoes, if using.
3 Leave the sauce to stand for a few hours before serving. It will keep in the fridge, in a screw-top jar, for 2–3 days, but is at its best when freshly made.

SAUCE CHIEN

(dog sauce)

I first encountered this bizarrely named sauce many years ago at the famous La Sammana Resort Hotel on the island of St Maarten in the Caribbean. The chef served it spooned over grilled fish and vegetables, but never could tell me how it got its name! My research since then suggests that it is named after the numerous packs of wild dogs that roam the island. In essence it is similar to a French vinaigrette but with the spirit and character of the French West Indies.

makes 150ml

2 garlic cloves, crushed
1 hot red chilli (habañero or Scotch bonnet)
2 shallots, finely chopped
3 spring onions, finely chopped
3 tablespoons chopped coriander
2 tablespoons chopped flat-leaf parsley
½ teaspoon chopped thyme leaves
salt and freshly cracked black pepper
juice of 2 limes
50ml olive oil
3 tablespoons boiling water

1 In a bowl, mix the garlic, chilli, shallots, spring onions, herbs and some salt and pepper.
2 Add the lime juice and whisk in the oil.
3 Add the boiling water and whisk to form a light emulsion, then adjust the seasoning. Leave to infuse for 1 hour before using. The sauce can be kept for 2 days, in a sealed container in the fridge.

CAESAR DRESSING

This classic dressing was first created in 1924 in Mexico, by the Italian chef Caesar Cardini at his restaurant in Tijuana. It has now emerged as an international icon, showing up in casual as well as high-end restaurants the world over.

The art of making a great Caesar dressing, and salad for that matter, is to strike the right balance: too much garlic is overpowering, for instance.

Those of you who are not fans of anchovies might like to know that the original recipe did not in fact include them. Sorry to say that mine does!

makes 250ml

1 large free-range egg
1 teaspoon Worcestershire sauce
juice of ½ lemon
1 garlic clove, crushed
4 salted anchovies, rinsed, dried and finely chopped
1 teaspoon superfine capers, rinsed and chopped
1 teaspoon Dijon mustard
freshly cracked black pepper
75ml extra virgin olive oil
40g Parmesan cheese (preferably Reggiano), finely grated

1 Immerse the egg in boiling water for 1 minute. Remove and leave to cool.
2 Mix the Worcestershire sauce, lemon juice, garlic, anchovies, capers and mustard in a bowl. Season with pepper.
3 Crack the egg into the bowl and whisk until smooth. Slowly trickle in the oil in a steady stream, whisking until smooth and emulsified. Do not add the oil too quickly or the sauce will separate.
4 Stir in the grated Parmesan and serve.

Variation

ROQUEFORT CAESAR DRESSING

Replace the Parmesan with crumbled Roquefort cheese.

TROPICAL ISLAND CHUTNEY

This is more of a sauce than a chutney, but made along the same lines. A lot of New World sauces include fruit, which is not surprising given how abundant fruit is in this part of the world.

makes 350ml

150ml cider vinegar
50g caster sugar
25g dark brown sugar
1 red onion, finely diced
1 hot red chilli, deseeded and diced
2.5cm piece of fresh ginger, peeled and grated
½ teaspoon ground cinnamon
½ teaspoon ground allspice
50g sultanas
1 ripe mango, peeled and cut into small dice
150g fresh pineapple, peeled and cut into small dice
1 guava, peeled and cut into small dice
1 banana, peeled and cut into small dice
2 teaspoons chopped coriander (optional)

1 Put the vinegar and both sugars in a heavy-based pan and bring slowly to the boil. Add the onion, chilli, ginger and spices and cook for a further 10 minutes.
2 Add the sultanas and diced fruits and cook over a low heat for a final 15 minutes. Leave to cool, and add the coriander, if using, before serving.

XNIPEC SALSA

This is a sweet and sour habañero chilli salsa from the Yucatán peninsula in Mexico. Habañero, usually red or yellow, is an extremely fiery chilli, often confused with the infamous Scotch bonnet, which is also lantern-shaped. Despite its intense heat it has a fruity tone that goes particularly well with fruits and tomatoes. Use it sparingly, and take care when handling it. If you prefer, use milder chillies.
⊕ *Lovely with grilled fish or chicken.*

makes 150ml

1 red onion, chopped
3 ripe vine tomatoes, peeled, deseeded and chopped
1 habañero chilli (or other red chilli), deseeded and chopped
100ml fresh sour (Seville) orange juice or half-and-half lime juice and orange juice
salt

1 Combine all the ingredients in a bowl, with salt to taste, and leave for 30 minutes, for the flavours to infuse.

PG tip Seville oranges are widely available for a short season in winter, but can sometimes be found at other times in Hispanic grocery shops. If you can't get them, use ordinary oranges, but add a little lime juice to give that sour effect.

मोयाबसस्टेण्ड.बड़ी
सीमेन्ट
रेती

ASIA

The sauces of Asia are usually based on a few simple ingredients and are quick and easy to prepare. Throughout the region you'll find a plethora of dipping sauces placed on practically every table, both in the home and in restaurants. They make a wonderful accompaniment to finger foods such as crisp spring rolls and grilled spiced meat satays, or spooned over local delicacies such as seafood and fish salads. These sauces may have a thin consistency but are full of spice and savour. Extremely versatile, they can be used to enliven a simple dish of noodles or rice, and make everyday meals memorable. They are also a boon for the busy cook, as they require little, if any, cooking and often rely on store-cupboard ingredients.

Some Asian sauces form an integral part of the dish and are slightly more complex. Thai, Malaysian and Indian curry sauces, for example, require a spice paste to be prepared first by roasting and pounding spices and aromatics; the paste is then added to coconut milk or stock and used for cooking meat, fish or vegetables. Like the simplest of dipping sauces, however, these cooking sauces are always characterised by clear, vibrant flavours.

BALINESE DARK SOY SAUCE

A fiery-hot, salty sauce that will enliven the palate, with shades of liquorice from the kecap manis. ⊕ *Serve with satays or use as a dressing for seafood salad.*

makes 150ml

½ garlic clove, peeled
3 tablespoons vegetable oil
1 teaspoon finely chopped lemon grass
2 spring onions, finely chopped
4 tablespoons kecap manis (Indonesian soy sauce)
1 hot red chilli, finely chopped
1 teaspoon distilled white vinegar

1 Pound the garlic in a mortar to a paste.
2 Heat the oil in a small frying pan, add the pounded garlic, stir-fry for 1–2 seconds, then transfer to a small bowl.
3 Add the remaining ingredients to the bowl and leave to stand for 15 minutes to let the flavours infuse.

PG tip Kecap manis is a sweet-based soy sauce, almost liquorice in flavour. It is used widely in Indonesian cookery, and as a seasoning or condiment. If you can't find it, reduce equal quantities of light soy sauce and treacle with a good pinch of ground star anise in a pan until lightly thickened.

SRIRACHA SAUCE

Sriracha is the generic name for the hot sauce adorning every Southeast Asian restaurant table. Like many sauces of the region, it has a perfect balance of sweetness and spice.

Although it started life in a Thai port called Sri Racha, I first encountered the sauce in California, on hot-dog vendor stalls and taco stands, served like a ketchup – the perfect accompaniment! Such is its global popularity now that commercial brands are readily available, but it's very simple, and much better, to make your own. ⊕ *It adds a warm glow to seafood such as oysters and clams.*

makes 350ml

175g hot red chillies, chopped
1 tablespoon tomato purée
125ml distilled white vinegar
75g sugar
6 garlic cloves, crushed
200g tinned tomatoes

1 Put the chillies and tomato purée in a pan with the vinegar and sugar, and bring to the boil.
2 Add the garlic and tomatoes and cook for 10 minutes.
3 Transfer to a blender and blitz until smooth, then leave to go cold before serving. It can be kept in the fridge in a sealed container for up to 1 month.

Variation

COCKTAIL SAUCE

Add 2 tablespoons sriracha to 4 tablespoons mayonnaise and use for a great Asian-style prawn cocktail sauce, or serve with fried calamari.

NAM PRIK PHAO

(roasted chilli sauce)

In Thailand, this fragrant and spicy-hot sauce makes the perfect accompaniment to many dishes: stirred into fried rice with vegetables or seafood or, the way I like it, brushed over grilled fish or shellfish.

makes 300ml

100ml vegetable oil
4 shallots, sliced
4 garlic cloves, crushed
8 small dried red chillies
1 tablespoon dried shrimp paste
1 tablespoon palm sugar or brown sugar (optional)
3 tablespoons nam pla (Thai fish sauce)
2 tablespoons tamarind paste
salt

1 Heat the oil in a wok or large frying pan and add the shallots and garlic. Cook until lightly golden, then remove with a slotted spoon to a blender.
2 Add the chillies and shrimp paste to the wok or pan and fry for 1 minute. Remove with a slotted spoon to the blender, reserving the oil in the wok.
3 Add the sugar, if using, to the blender and blitz. Add the nam pla, tamarind, some salt and the reserved oil from the wok, then blitz again to a blended purée.
4 Transfer to a bowl and leave to cool. Serve cold. It can be refrigerated for up to three months.

PG tip – a word on fish sauce
Don't be put off by the pungent aroma. Incorporated into a sauce, dressing or curry, fish sauce becomes less powerful, quite addictive and a healthy alternative to salt. The Vietnamese (nuoc mam) and Thai (nam pla) versions, made from fermented anchovies, prawns or squid, are considered the best and are widely available. Once opened, fish sauce should be refrigerated.

PAN-ROASTED MUSSELS WITH ROASTED CHILLI SAUCE

serves 4

2 tablespoons vegetable oil
2 garlic cloves, crushed
2 tablespoons nam prik phao (see left)
1kg fresh mussels, debearded and cleaned
2 tablespoons nam pla (Thai fish sauce)
100ml oyster sauce
2 large red chillies, sliced
12 Thai sweet basil leaves
150ml chicken stock (see page 9)
a pinch of sugar, to taste

1 Heat the oil in a wok or large frying pan, add the garlic and nam prik phao and cook for 30 seconds.
2 Add the mussels in their shells and stir-fry for 1 minute in the sauce.
3 Add the remaining ingredients and cook for a further 2–3 minutes, or until the mussels have opened.
4 Divide between 4 bowls and serve with steamed rice.

PG tip When preparing molluscs of any sort, ensure they are closed. Any with open shells are dead and can cause food poisoning. Again, once they are cooked, any remaining closed are dead; discard them too.

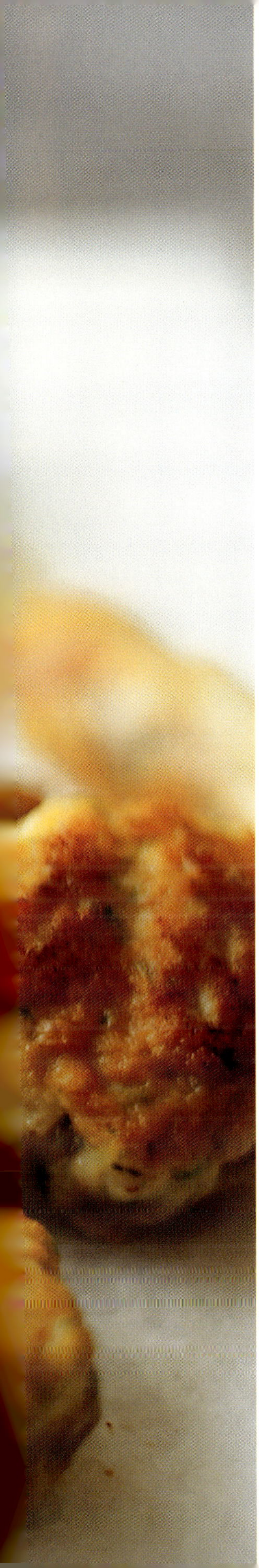

THAI DIPPING SAUCE

I could devour this delicate sweet-and-sour sauce by the gallon. ⊕ *Traditionally served with Thai appetisers such as satays, spring rolls and spicy fish cakes.*

makes 300ml

4 tablespoons distilled white vinegar
120g sugar
120ml water
1 tablespoon nam pla (Thai fish sauce)
1 small red chilli, finely sliced
1.5cm piece of fresh ginger, peeled and finely chopped (optional)
100g cucumber, finely diced
2 tablespoons chopped roasted peanuts

1 Put the vinegar, sugar, water, nam pla, chilli and ginger, if using, in a pan and bring to the boil.
2 Simmer, uncovered, for 5 minutes or until slightly thickened.
3 Stir in the cucumber and peanuts and serve at room temperature.

CHILLI VINEGAR DIPPING SAUCE

This sauce was on almost every table wherever I ate in Thailand, although you will find a version of it throughout Asia; it is a sharply flavoured condiment that enlivens any dish. ⊕ *I particularly enjoy it with stir-fried noodles or rice dishes.*

makes 150ml

2 hot red chillies, thinly sliced
100ml distilled white vinegar
2 teaspoons nam pla (Thai fish sauce)

1 Combine the ingredients in a bowl and leave to stand for 15 minutes to allow the flavours to infuse. The dip will keep for 2 weeks in a sealed container in the fridge.

NAM PRIK NOOM

(green chilli dipping sauce)

A very hot dip served with sticky rice or grilled vegetables. Charring the ingredients on a barbecue improves the flavour no end, but a grill pan does an acceptable job.

makes 300ml

6 garlic cloves
6 green chillies
100g large banana shallots, halved lengthways
4 ripe, firm tomatoes, deseeded and diced
100ml vegetable oil
2 tablespoon nam pla (Thai fish sauce)
juice of 2 limes
2 tablespoons chopped coriander
a good pinch of sugar

1 Heat a dry grill pan over a high heat and add the garlic, chillies and shallots. Fry for 4–5 minutes, stirring, until fragrant, then leave to cool before cutting them into small chunks.

2 Transfer to a mortar with the tomatoes. Using a pestle, grind to a paste.

3 Add the oil, nam pla, lime juice, coriander and sugar and mix well.

NUOC MAM CHAM

(Vietnamese dipping sauce)

No meal in Vietnam is considered complete without this sauce; it is used as freely as we use salt and pepper. Endless variations are found across Asia, Malaysia, Cambodia and Thailand. ⊕ *As with all Asian-style dipping sauces, this is great for serving with grilled meat and fish, vegetables and crispy spring rolls.*

makes 200ml

125ml water or coconut juice
2 tablespoons rice wine vinegar
2 tablespoons palm sugar or caster sugar
2 garlic cloves, crushed
4 hot red chillies, preferably bird's-eye, finely chopped
1 teaspoon lemon or lime juice
2 tablespoons nuoc mam (Vietnamese fish sauce)

1 Put the water or coconut juice in a small pan with the vinegar and sugar and bring to the boil. Remove from the heat and set aside to cool.

2 Add the garlic, chillies and lemon or lime juice, then stir in the nuoc mam.

Variations

Add one of the following to the basic sauce: shredded radish or carrots, carrot pickles, chopped coriander, a little chopped fresh ginger or chopped lemon grass.

NUOC LEO

A cousin of nuoc mam cham; use in the same way. Put 1 tablespoon nuoc mam cham (see above) into a bowl and add 4 tablespoons hoisin sauce, 3 tablespoons water, 1 tablespoon sweet chilli sauce (see page 146) and 2 tablespoons finely ground dry-roasted peanuts. Stir well to mix.

NAM JIM

(green chilli and coriander sauce)

A wonderful dressing, simple and addictive, one of the staples of the Thai kitchen and a great way of learning about the balance of flavour in Thai cooking. There is a number of variations, but the key elements remain the same: hot, sour, salty and sweet – exemplified here by chilli, garlic, lime juice, fish sauce and palm sugar, all the hallmarks of the country's cuisine. This recipe calls for coriander roots, but if they are unavailable, just use the leaves. ⊕ *Great for enlivening salads, as for my grilled pork and fennel salad, opposite.*

makes 200ml

1 tablespoon sea salt
3 garlic cloves
3 shallots, chopped
a good handful of coriander leaves, plus the scraped and cleaned roots
4 small hot green chillies, deseeded and chopped
3 tablespoons palm sugar or brown sugar
3 tablespoons nam pla (Thai fish sauce)
juice of 8 limes

1 Put the salt, garlic, shallots and coriander leaves and roots in a mortar and pestle, and pound until crushed.

2 Add the chillies and sugar and pound again, then remove to a bowl.

3 Add the nam pla and lime juice and mix thoroughly. The dressing should taste hot, sweet, sour and salty. Add more palm sugar to make it sweeter or more nam pla to make it more salty.

Variations

Replace the green chillies with Dutch or Indonesian lombok chillies, for a slightly less hot version.

SWEET THAI DRESSING

Add 2 tablespoons sweet chilli sauce (see page 146) to the basic recipe. Great with grilled beef or calamari salad.

GRILLED PORK NECK WITH FENNEL SALAD

serves 4

450g piece of pork neck, cleaned of all fat and sinew
3 teaspoons oyster sauce
2 large heads of fennel, outer layer removed
2 tablespoons olive oil
2 large shallots, thinly sliced
4 tablespoons nam jim (see opposite)
15g small mint leaves
2 tablespoons roughly chopped peanuts

1 Place the pork in a steamer set over a pan of simmering water and steam, covered, for 40 minutes until cooked. Remove to a chopping board and cut into 1.5cm cubes.
2 Put the pork in a bowl or shallow dish and add the oyster sauce. Mix well and leave to marinate for up to 1 hour.
3 Meanwhile, slice the fennel very thinly, using a kitchen mandolin if possible, then tip into iced water.
4 Heat a grill pan until very hot and brush with the oil. Drain the marinated pork pieces and add them to the hot pan. Cook for 2–3 minutes on each side, until lightly browned.
5 Drain and dry the fennel, then put in a bowl with the shallots. Add the nam jim and toss to mix.
6 Add the grilled pork, toss to coat, then divide the mixture between 4 individual serving plates.
7 Scatter over the mint leaves and peanuts and serve immediately.

ROASTED TOMATO AND GARLIC DIPPING SAUCE

In Laos, many sauces are flavoured with garlic, tomato and peppers and are infused with fresh herbs such as basil, coriander and mint.

makes 200ml

4 large garlic cloves, unpeeled
3 red chillies, halved lengthways
4 ripe but firm tomatoes, halved
1 small red pepper, halved and deseeded
2 tablespoons vegetable oil
2 tablespoons nam pla (Thai fish sauce)
4 tablespoons chopped coriander
2 spring onions, finely chopped
2 tablespoons chopped mint
juice of ½ lime

1 Preheat the oven to 200°C/400°F/gas mark 6. Put the garlic, chillies, tomatoes and red pepper in an oven dish or roasting tin and drizzle over the oil.
2 Roast in the oven for 20 minutes, then turn the vegetables and return to the oven for a further 20 minutes. Remove from the oven and leave to cool.
3 When they are cool, slip the roasted garlic cloves from their skin and put in a mortar with the roasted chillies and red pepper. Pound to a coarse paste.
4 Remove and discard the skin from the tomatoes, chop the flesh and add to the paste, then pound again to a paste.
5 Add the remaining ingredients, mix well and serve.

PG tip This sauce cannot be made very far in advance, as it relies on the flavour of freshly cooked ingredients. Make it a few hours before you need it, for the best results.

ROASTED TOMATO AND GARLIC DIPPING SAUCE

I particularly like this sauce served with steamed prawns or fish cooked wrapped in banana leaves, or, during the height of summer, cooked on a hot charcoal barbecue.

SPICE ISLANDS FRUIT SALSA WITH PEANUTS

A wonderful dip for raw vegetables, grilled fish or meat – easy to make and extremely tasty. Sometimes the sauce is blended to a purée, but I prefer it like this, with each ingredient's flavour shining through individually. ⊕ *Serve with prawn crackers – very moreish!*

makes 300ml

1 tablespoon vegetable oil
4 spring onions, finely chopped
1 ripe mango, peeled and diced
1 kaffir lime leaf
juice of 2 limes
100g fresh or tinned pineapple, diced
1 tablespoon palm sugar
75g roasted unsalted peanuts, chopped
3 tablespoons chopped coriander leaves
1 teaspoon sambal oelek (see page 148)

1 Mix all the ingredients in a bowl, adding a little more sambal oelek if you prefer a hotter salsa.

YELLOW PLUM SAUCE

Yellow plum sauce is yet another dipping sauce found in Thailand, traditionally enjoyed with fried foods, such as deep-fried shrimp cakes. Yellow plums have a short season, so enjoy them while you can.

makes 200ml

200g yellow plums, stoned and chopped
1 onion, chopped
3 small red chillies, deseeded and finely chopped
2.5cm piece of fresh ginger, peeled and chopped
100g sugar
100ml distilled white vinegar
200ml water
juice of 2 limes
a pinch of sea salt

1 Put all the ingredients in a pan and slowly bring to the boil. Reduce the heat a little and gently cook until the plums break down to a jam-like consistency.

2 Leave to cool and serve at room temperature.

RAITA

A soothing, yoghurt-based sauce, ideal to temper hot dishes such as curries. ⊕ In India it accompanies almost every dish.

makes 200ml

200g cucumber
½ teaspoon sea salt
150ml thick natural yoghurt
½ teaspoon sugar
2 tablespoons roughly chopped mint
a pinch of ground cumin

1 Grate the cucumber into a bowl, using a hand grater, add the salt and mix well. Spread the cucumber out on a tea towel, gather up the towel and squeeze out all the excess moisture.

2 Put the cucumber in a bowl and add the yoghurt, sugar, mint and cumin. Mix well and chill until ready to serve.

Variations

MANGO AND TOMATO RAITA

Replace the cucumber with 1 ripe, firm tomato and 1 small mango, both cut into small dice. Lovely with cold lobster and other seafood.

COCONUT AND GINGER RAITA

Add to the basic raita recipe a 2.5cm piece of fresh ginger, peeled and finely grated, and 2 tablespoons unsweetened desiccated coconut.

CORIANDER AND GREEN CHILLI RAITA

Omit the cucumber and replace the mint with fresh coriander and 2 finely chopped small green chillies. Great with grilled meats, especially burgers.

POMEGRANATE RAITA

Omit the cucumber from the main recipe, then fold in the seeds from 1 fresh pomegranate. A wonderful, refreshing dip in summer.

SPINACH RAITA

Blanch 150g young spinach leaves in boiling water for 30 seconds, then quickly plunge into iced water. Squeeze out excess moisture. Fry in a little oil with ½ garlic clove and 1 teaspoon cumin seeds, leave to cool, then chop finely. Add 200ml natural yoghurt, 2 tablespoons chopped mint and a squeeze of lemon. Great with pulses, as in the recipe below.

CHICKPEA CAKES WITH SPINACH RAITA

⊕ I love these vegetarian patties, either with raita as here, or tucked inside hot toasted pitta breads. I often serve them atop large, grilled portobello mushrooms – absolutely delicious.

serves 4

500g cooked dried chickpeas (or tinned, well drained)
3 free-range eggs
2 spring onions, finely chopped
3 tablespoons tahini (sesame seed paste)
1 small onion, finely chopped
½ garlic clove, crushed
2 tablespoons olive oil
75g fresh white breadcrumbs
3 tablespoons chopped coriander
salt and freshly cracked black pepper
200ml spinach raita (see above), to serve

1 Blitz the chickpeas, eggs, spring onions and tahini in a blender, then transfer to a mixing bowl.

2 Sweat the onions and garlic in half the oil until softened. Add to the chickpea mixture with the breadcrumbs and coriander. Season and mix well.

3 Using your hands, form into 8 equal-sized patties, then put them in the fridge to set for up to 1 hour.

4 Heat the remaining oil in a large, non-stick frying pan. Cook the patties 4 at a time until golden all over, about 4–5 minutes. Serve immediately with the spinach raita.

CORIANDER CHUTNEY

This basic Indian-style chutney can be made either raw or cooked, and I include both versions here. ⊕ *Either way, it makes a great dipping sauce for serving with grilled lamb cutlets, crispy spicy samosas or simply with poppadoms.*

for the raw chutney
makes 200ml

100g coriander, stalks included
2 hot green chillies, chopped
2.5cm piece of fresh ginger, peeled and grated
2 garlic cloves
½ teaspoon ground cumin
juice of ½ lemon
½ teaspoon salt
½ teaspoon sugar
50ml coconut milk or natural yoghurt

1 Put all the ingredients except for the coconut milk or yoghurt in a blender and blitz to a coarse purée.
2 Add the coconut milk or yoghurt and blitz again until smooth, then transfer to a jar or covered bowl and refrigerate. The raw chutney will keep in the fridge for 2–3 days.

for the cooked chutney
makes 200ml

100ml vegetable oil
2 hot green chillies, chopped
100g coriander, stalks included
salt
75ml water
½ teaspoon black mustard seeds
½ teaspoon ground cumin
2 tablespoons urad dhal (black lentils)
4 curry leaves

1 Heat half the oil in a pan, add the chillies and coriander and fry for 30 seconds. Remove from the heat and leave to cool.
2 When the mixture is cool, transfer to a small blender with a little salt and the water, and blitz to a paste.
3 Heat the remaining oil in a pan and add the mustard seeds, cumin and urad dhal. When it begins to splutter, add the curry leaves with the chilli and coriander mixture and cook for 10–20 seconds, just long enough to infuse the flavours.
4 Transfer to the blender and blitz until smooth. Leave to cool before serving. The cooked chutney will keep for 2–3 days in a sealed jar in the fridge.

BLATJANG

(dried fruit chutney sauce)

Blatjang is rather like a chutney, but with a smoother consistency. ⊕ *It is wonderful with cold meat cuts, but I particularly like it served with cheese, especially washed-rind Époisse, or creamy blue-veined Stilton.*

makes 1 litre

400g mixed dried fruit such as fig, apricot and pear, soaked in water until softened
75g raisins
1 onion, finely chopped
1 hot red chilli, finely chopped (or more, according to taste)
2 garlic cloves, crushed
750ml water
1 tablespoon ground ginger
½ tablespoon ground coriander
½ teaspoon ground cinnamon
50ml distilled white vinegar
100g soft brown sugar
salt and a pinch of cayenne pepper

1 Cut the dried fruit into small pieces, about 1cm across.

2 Put all the ingredients in a heavy-based pan and quickly bring to the boil.

3 Lower the heat and simmer, uncovered, for 45 minutes–1 hour, until the fruits are thick, syrupy and broken up into a pulp. Add a little more water during the cooking process if the sauce becomes too thick.

SWEET CHILLI SAUCE

This Thai sauce has a wonderful, distinctive flavour: it's intensely thick and sweet, with a copious amount of garlic. Bird's-eye chillies are fiery little numbers and really add a punch to southern Asian foods. If you can't find them, use the smallest ones available – this generally means the hottest.

makes 300ml

8 bird's-eye chillies, half of them puréed in a small blender, the rest finely chopped
100ml hot water
225g sugar
100ml distilled white vinegar
6 large garlic cloves, crushed
1 teaspoon salt
1 tablespoon nam pla (Thai fish sauce)
juice of 1 small lime

1 Put the chillies in a pan, pour over the hot water and leave to soften for 20 minutes.
2 Once the chillies have softened, heat them in their soaking water, then add the sugar, vinegar, garlic and salt and bring to the boil.
3 Simmer for 12–15 minutes, until syrupy.
4 Stir in the nam pla and lime juice, then leave to cool at room temperature. Keep the sauce in a tightly sealed jar, stored at room temperature for up to 1 month.

Variation

MANGO KERABU

For a Malaysian-style variation to serve with fried rice as a side dish, add 1 diced small mango and 2 tablespoons each of chopped coriander and mint to 4 tablespoons of the finished sweet chilli sauce.

PG tip If you want a thicker sauce, 'slake' it by stirring 1 teaspoon cornflour with 1 tablespoon water and adding it to the finished sauce. I love this sauce; I use it like tomato ketchup. Try adding a couple of spoonfuls to mayonnaise with a little grated fresh ginger and serving it with fish and chips – heaven!

TOMATO AND COCONUT SAMBAL

The word sambal is prevalent in the vocabulary of India and many South Asian and Pacific Rim countries. In Sri Lanka, sambals are often a little milder as they include coconut milk, whereas further east they pack a more fiery power. ⊕ *This particular version is served warm and is fantastic with grilled fish, especially on a bed of cinnamon-steamed jasmine rice.*

makes 350ml

2 tablespoons vegetable oil
1 shallot, thinly sliced
2 green chillies, finely chopped (or finely sliced if you are using a thinner variety of chilli)
2.5cm piece of fresh ginger, peeled and grated
1 garlic clove, sliced
2 teaspoons mild curry powder
6 curry leaves
200g cherry tomatoes
100ml coconut cream
juice of 2 limes
10 Thai sweet basil leaves
salt

1 Heat the oil in a wok or frying pan and add shallot, chillies, ginger and garlic. Cook over a low heat for 4–5 minutes.
2 Add the curry powder, curry leaves and tomatoes and cook for 2–3 minutes.
3 Pour in the coconut cream and lime juice, and cook for a final 5 minutes.
4 Stir in the basil, season and serve.

SAMBAL OELEK

This Indonesian-inspired chilli sauce is to Asian dishes what harissa is to Moroccan: a little spoonful adds a spice kick and enlivens food in seconds.

⊕ *Serve with meat, or add to stir-fries and fried rice. I often add a little to a pizza base and top it with barbecued chicken, for an Asian-style pizza.*

makes 200ml

2 garlic cloves, crushed
½ teaspoon dried shrimp paste (terasi or blachan)
1 teaspoon salt
4 large red chillies, chopped
1 teaspoon sugar
2 limes, peeled and cut into small pieces
4 tablespoons hot water
1 tablespoon rice wine vinegar
100ml nam pla (Thai fish sauce)
2 tablespoons Thai sweet basil leaves

1 Put the garlic, shrimp paste, salt and chillies in a mortar and pound to a coarse paste with a pestle. (This can be done in a blender if you prefer.)

2 Add the sugar, limes, water, vinegar and nam pla, and pound (or blend) to a thick paste. Add the sweet basil leaves and pound (or blend) again. Store in a sealed container in the fridge for up to 1 month.

Variations

TOMATO SAMBAL

From neighbouring Bali, this is great served with barbecued fish. Add 20g finely chopped tomatoes to the basic recipe.

LEMON GRASS AND SHALLOT SAMBAL

Add 4 very finely chopped sticks of lemon grass (outer husk removed) and 2 chopped shallots to the basic recipe.

INDONESIAN SWEET POTATO SOUP

The natural sweetness in sweet potato makes it the perfect vegetable for this Asian-inspired soup, which I first prepared many years ago for an American guest who requested a spicy hot soup flavoured with coconut. This is my result – and it went down a treat!

serves 4

1 litre well-flavoured chicken stock (see page 9)
4 sticks of lemon grass, outer husks removed, chopped
200ml sambal oelek (see left)
20g coriander leaves and stalks, separated
5cm piece of galangal or fresh ginger, peeled and chopped
2 sweet potatoes, peeled and cut into small chunks
150ml coconut milk
1 tablespoon nam pla (Thai fish sauce)

1 Put the chicken stock, lemon grass, sambal oelek and coriander stalks in a pan and bring to the boil. Reduce to a simmer and cook for 10 minutes.

2 Add the galangal or ginger and the sweet potatoes to the pan and simmer for 15 minutes, or until very soft. Remove from the heat and leave to cool slightly.

3 Transfer to a blender and blitz until smooth, then strain into a clean pan.

4 Add the coconut milk and nam pla and simmer for 5 minutes. Stir in the coriander leaves and serve.

ACHIN

(garlic and ginger fish sauce)

The food of Burma reflects the influences of the country's many neighbours, especially the largest, India and China. Indian influences can be seen in the use of tamarind, and Chinese in the abundance of ginger, garlic and soy sauce. ⊕ *I recently tasted this sauce while visiting the Burmese-Thai border, where it was served with crisp tempura-fried vegetables.*

makes 150ml

2 garlic cloves, chopped
2.5cm piece of fresh ginger, peeled and chopped
4 tablespoons tamarind paste
4 tablespoons honey
1 teaspoon sugar
1 tablespoon soy sauce
2 teaspoons nam pla (Thai fish sauce)
1 small red pepper, chopped
a pinch each of salt and paprika

1 Pound the garlic and ginger in a mortar (or blender) to a fine paste, then transfer to a bowl.
2 Add the remaining ingredients and stir to form a smooth sauce. It can be kept in a sealed container in the fridge for up to 7 days.

ASIAN GINGER DRESSING

⊕ *A terrific dressing for steamed fish or shellfish, and also great for Asian-style vegetable salads.*

makes 150ml

2 tablespoons nam pla (Thai fish sauce)
2 tablespoons water
2 tablespoons rice wine vinegar
2 tablespoons light soy sauce
2 teaspoons sugar
10 mint leaves
1 shallot, finely chopped
2.5cm piece of fresh ginger, peeled and grated
salt and freshly cracked black pepper

1 Mix all the ingredients in a bowl with salt and pepper to taste and leave to infuse for 1 hour. This sauce will keep only for 1–2 days in the fridge; after that it will lose its freshness of flavour.

THAI CURRY SAUCE

There are some perfectly acceptable prepared red and green pastes on the market, but to my mind they don't compare with those made at home.

Authentic Thai sauces are made by first producing a spice paste, either red, using dried red chillies, or green, using fresh green chillies. The green is hotter and more sour in flavour than the red, but both are delicious.

Nobby-looking galangal, with its almost camphorised scent and flavour, is similar to root ginger, but really does add a different flavour to the sauce. It is available from Asian grocers, but fresh root ginger is an acceptable substitute. The paste will keep perfectly well in a sealed container in the fridge for up to 2 months.

makes 750ml

for red curry paste

1 tablespoon coriander seeds
1 tablespoon cumin seeds
10 dried red chillies (or fresh)
1 teaspoon dried shrimp paste (terasi or blachan)
3 shallots, chopped
2.5cm piece of fresh galangal or ginger, chopped
3 sticks of lemon grass, outer husks removed, finely chopped
4 kaffir lime leaves, torn
grated zest of 1 lime
2 tablespoons coriander stalks or leaves chopped

1 Heat a heavy-based frying pan over a high heat, add the coriander and cumin seeds and quickly brown until golden, stirring constantly.

2 Transfer to a mortar or blender, add the remaining ingredients and pound or blitz to a smooth paste; it may be necessary to scrape down the sides of the blender, if using, during the process.

for the curry sauce

1 tablespoon vegetable oil
400ml tinned unsweetened coconut cream
2 tablespoons red or green curry paste (see left and above)
800ml tinned unsweetened coconut milk
2 tablespoons nam pla (Thai fish sauce)
4 kaffir lime leaves, torn

1 Heat the oil in a heavy-based pan, add the coconut cream and cook for 15–20 minutes until it splits (separates).

2 Add the curry paste, cook for 10 minutes, then add the coconut milk, nam pla and lime leaves and simmer for 20 minutes. The sauce is now ready for use in the recipe of your choice.

Variations

GREEN CURRY PASTE

Replace the red chillies with the same amount of bird's-eye green chillies and proceed in the same way as for red.

LEMON-GRASS CURRY PASTE

For a lemon-grass curry sauce from neighbouring Cambodia, add 6 finely chopped lemon grass stalks, a pinch of ground turmeric and 1 teaspoon dried shrimp paste to a basic green curry sauce as it cooks.

MINTED PEA AUBERGINE AND BEAN CURRY

Pea aubergines are an Asian variety of aubergine and, as their name suggests, are pea-shaped and about the size of a large grape. They are very bitter, and add a tart, astringent flavour to the curry.

serves 4

150g green beans
2 tablespoons vegetable or groundnut oil
4 green chillies, thinly sliced
5cm piece of fresh ginger, peeled and thinly sliced
225g pea aubergines (see above)
600ml Thai green curry sauce (see opposite)
125g shelled broad beans (frozen or fresh)
4 ripe, firm tomatoes, chopped
1 tablespoon tamarind paste
50g small fresh mint leaves
steamed jasmine or basmati rice, to serve

1 Blanch the green beans in boiling, salted water for 2–3 minutes, then refresh in cold water and dry them.
2 Heat the oil in a wok over a moderate heat and add the chillies and ginger. Fry until lightly softened, 2–3 minutes.
3 Add the pea aubergines, then the green curry sauce, and cook for 5 minutes.
4 Add the blanched green beans, broad beans and tomatoes, and cook for a further 5–8 minutes.
5 Stir in the tamarind and the mint leaves, and serve over the steamed rice.

TAMARIND SAUCE

Tamarind, from the pods of the tamarind tree, is a distinctive souring agent. It can be purchased in block form (pulp) or as a concentrate or paste.

⊕ *This sauce is great with crispy-fried samosas as a dip, or with other Indian snacks such as bhel poori. It also makes a wonderful glaze for barbecued chicken as it cooks, or for fried fish.*

makes 400ml

150g block tamarind pulp, chopped
1 small, red bird's-eye chilli
2.5cm piece of fresh ginger, peeled and chopped
50g soft light brown sugar or 2 tablespoons honey
1 tablespoon soy sauce
1 garlic clove, crushed

1 Soak the tamarind pulp in 300ml boiling water for 2 hours, or until soft. (If you are in a hurry, simmer the tamarind in the water in a pan for 20 minutes.)
2 Pour the pulp into a sieve set over a clean pan and push it through, using a wooden spoon.
3 Add the remaining ingredients and 150ml cold water, then bring to the boil and simmer for 5 minutes.
4 Leave to cool, adding a little more sugar to taste if necessary. Store in a sealed container in the fridge for up to 4 days, or frozen for up to 3 months.

Variations

ORANGE-TAMARIND SAUCE

Replace the cold water in step 3 with the juice and grated zest of 1 orange; lovely with roast duck.

MINT TAMARIND

Add 2 tablespoons mint sauce (see page 72) to the finished sauce.

TAMARIND KETCHUP

Mix half the sauce with an equal amount of tomato ketchup and add 2 tablespoons chopped coriander.

INDONESIAN PEANUT SAUCE

Peanut sauces can be found in many Asian and Pacific Rim cuisines, generally served with satays and spring rolls. In Indonesia, they tend to be spicier than further east, with a little curry paste added.

makes 400ml

1 tablespoon vegetable oil
1 shallot, finely chopped
2 garlic cloves, crushed
200ml coconut milk
2 teaspoons red curry paste (see page 150)
1 teaspoon dried shrimp paste (terasi or blachan; optional)
2 teaspoons sugar
125ml water
100g crunchy peanut butter
2 teaspoons kecap manis (Indonesian soy sauce)
a drizzle of hot chilli oil (optional), to serve

1 Heat the oil in a heavy pan and add the shallot and garlic. Cook for 4–5 minutes until softened.
2 Add the coconut milk and bring to the boil. Stir in the curry paste, shrimp paste, if using, and sugar.
3 Whisk in the water and peanut butter, lower the heat and add the kecap manis. Simmer for 1 minute, then transfer the sauce to a dish and serve warm, drizzled with a little chilli oil, if using. Kept in the fridge in a sealed container, this sauce will last for 3–4 days.

GADO GADO

The beauty of this Indonesian vegetable salad lies both in its simplicity and the variation of textures in the vegetables. Sometimes it also includes tofu, which is a handy addition for vegetarians. If you have an egg slicer, use it here for thin, even slices.

serves 4

1 tablespoon mango chutney
200ml Indonesian peanut sauce (see left)
200g baby new potatoes, boiled and cooled
2 small carrots, thinly sliced in rounds and lightly cooked
50g cooked green beans, cut into small lengths
50g bean sprouts
¼ cucumber, halved lengthways and sliced
2 tomatoes, each cut into 4 slices
salt and freshly cracked black pepper
2 free-range eggs, hard-boiled, peeled and thinly sliced
2 tablespoons roughly chopped roasted peanuts

1 In a large bowl, stir the mango chutney into the peanut sauce. Add the potatoes, carrots, beans, bean sprouts, cucumber and tomatoes, with salt and pepper to taste, and mix well.
2 Put a stainless-steel ring or 7.5cm cookie cutter on a plate, then fill it with the salad, pressing it down lightly to compact.
3 Remove the ring or cutter, decorate the top with overlapping egg slices and sprinkle with peanuts.
4 Repeat the ring/cookie cutter process on 3 more plates and serve at room temperature.

PG tip Many good cook shops sell stainless-steel rings, but otherwise a small baked-bean tin opened at both ends makes a perfect mould for use in the kitchen.

99
49

THE PACIFIC rim

Clustered around the immense Pacific Ocean, this loose grouping of countries stretches from Vietnam, China and Japan all the way round to the American West Coast and has great culinary diversity. Japanese sauces tend to be highly concentrated, served in small amounts and designed to set off the flavour of exquisite morsels of food – perhaps a pungent wasabi sauce to go with sashimi, or ponzu, a sour dipping sauce made from soy and yuzu (an oriental citrus fruit), to accompany chilled shellfish – especially good with oysters. In China, too, sauces are light yet emphatic, often based on strong, salty, fermented foods such as soya and black beans, with ginger and garlic to refresh the flavour. This lightness of touch also characterises the cooking of the West Coast of America. With its chequered history, this area has absorbed culinary influences from Spain, Mexico, Italy and the immigrant Chinese population. Healthy foods such as salads and stir-fries reign supreme, and vinaigrettes and marinades often take the place of richer sauces.

ADOBO

Adobo is Spanish for marinade, and I have been lucky enough to taste different types across the globe. They all seem to vary in flavour, but in Mexico, heat is the major factor; in southern Asia they seem to have an acidic flavour too, but chilli is always the main ingredient.

Annatto, also known as achiote, which is the tree it comes from, is a reddish-brown seed, which can be bought whole or in powder form. It adds a wonderful orange colour, and is used widely as a natural food colouring.

makes 600ml

1 tablespoon vegetable oil
4 hot red chillies, roughly chopped
3 garlic cloves, crushed
2 tablespoons tomato purée
150ml white wine vinegar
250ml chicken stock (see page 8)
1 bay leaf
2 teaspoons crushed coriander seeds
1 teaspoon annatto powder (or seeds)
4 tablespoons soy sauce
½ teaspoon freshly cracked black peppercorns
1 teaspoon sugar
salt

1 Heat the oil in a frying pan, add the chillies and garlic and cook over a low heat until the chillies are lightly golden and blistered.

2 Add the tomato purée and cook for a further 3–4 minutes.

3 Transfer to a blender and add the remaining ingredients except the salt. Blitz until smooth, then return to the pan and cook over a low heat for 15–20 minutes.

4 Season to taste; the mixture should be slightly sweet and sour in flavour with a hint of saltiness. It will keep for several days in a sealed container in the fridge.

PORK STRIPS IN ADOBO

(for 4 people)

Put 750g boneless belly pork strips, cut into small pieces, in a shallow dish and pour over 300ml adobo sauce. Cover and leave to marinate in the fridge for 4 hours. Heat 2 tablespoons vegetable oil in a wok or large frying pan and quickly fry the marinated pork pieces until golden. Add the marinade to the wok, cover and cook for 5 minutes, stirring occasionally, or until the sauce has reduced slightly. Serve the pork in its sauce with steamed basmati or jasmine rice. You could also make this dish with chicken pieces instead of pork.

CHAR SUI

Whenever I visit London's Soho, I always take time out to visit the Chinese restaurants and, understandably, always buy and consume far too many char sui buns. They are out of this world: pork steamed in fluffy dough and bound inside in this sweet, sticky barbecue sauce. It's great too with barbecued meat, such as pork or chicken.

makes 300ml

50ml dry sherry
100ml hoisin sauce (see page 160 for homemade)
50ml light soy sauce
50g sugar
4 garlic cloves
1 tablespoon black bean paste
½ teaspoon Chinese five-spice powder
2 shallots, finely chopped
salt

1 Put all the ingredients, except the salt, in a pan and slowly bring to the boil.
2 Lower the heat and simmer, uncovered, for 10–12 minutes, or until thick. Add salt to taste and leave to cool completely before using.

CHINESE PEANUT SAUCE

Less spicy than the Indonesian version of the sauce (see page 153), *This is very good served with spring rolls or satays.*

makes 300ml

125ml chicken stock (see page 8)
4 tablespoons smooth or crunchy peanut butter, or 100g roasted peanuts
2 tablespoons light soy sauce
2 garlic cloves, crushed
1 tablespoon rice wine vinegar
3 teaspoons sugar
¼ teaspoon chilli powder
2 tablespoons chopped coriander leaves

1 Put the stock in a pan and bring to the boil. Add the peanut butter or peanuts, soy sauce and garlic and simmer for 2–3 minutes.
2 Transfer to a blender and add the vinegar, sugar, chilli powder and coriander.
3 Blitz to a coarse sauce-like consistency.

JAPANESE ROASTED SESAME SEED SAUCE

An extremely versatile sauce, but I love it best with fried rice; it adds an instant flavour burst. ⊕ *It also makes an excellent dipping sauce and goes very with most vegetables, especially green beans or broccoli.*

makes 200ml

120g Japanese white sesame seeds (see tip below)
1 tablespoon sesame oil
1 tablespoon vegetable oil
150ml shoyu (Japanese soy sauce)
2 tablespoons mirin (Japanese sweet rice wine)
1 tablespoon brown sugar
½ teaspoon dashi (see page 9) mixed with 100ml warm water

1 Heat a dry frying pan or wok over a high heat and, when it is almost smoking, add the sesame seeds and fry until golden, keeping the seeds moving to prevent them burning. Transfer to a mortar.
2 Add both oils and crush the seeds to a paste with a pestle.
3 Stir in the shoyu, mirin, sugar and dashi and water mixture, transfer to a bowl and refrigerate until needed. It is best eaten within 1–2 days.

PG tip Japanese sesame seeds, known as gomaiso, are plumper than normal sesame seeds, and have a nuttier, more complex flavour. They are available from Asian stores, but if you can't find them, ordinary ones will do here.

SICHUAN SAUCE

The Sichuan region of China is noted for its gastronomy, and for its fiery dishes and sauces in particular. This classic chilli sauce is wonderful with stir-fried noodles and vegetables, or sprinkled over steamed fragrant rice. There are recipes for tomato ketchup and hoisin sauce elsewhere in this book, if you want to make your own, but bottled will be fine here.

makes 400ml

2 tablespoons tomato ketchup (see page 167 for homemade)
2 tablespoons hoisin sauce (see page 160 for homemade)
2 tablespoons black bean sauce
1 tablespoon plum sauce
2 tablespoons Shaoxing wine or dry sherry
2 teaspoons Chinese black vinegar
2 teaspoons chilli paste
2 tablespoons light soy sauce
2 tablespoons groundnut oil
2 garlic cloves, crushed
5cm piece of fresh ginger, peeled and grated
150ml chicken stock (see page 8)
2 teaspoons sesame oil

1 Put the ketchup, hoisin sauce, black bean sauce, plum sauce, wine or sherry, vinegar, chilli paste and soy sauce in a bowl.
2 Heat the groundnut oil in a wok or frying pan and add the garlic and ginger. Cook for 1 minute, then add the mixture in the bowl to the pan, with the stock. Cook for 4–5 minutes, remove from the heat, add the sesame oil and serve.

HOISIN SAUCE

Also known as Peking sauce, hoisin sauce is a thick, reddish-brown Chinese dipping sauce with a flavour best described as a blend of sweet, salty and spicy overtones. Made from fermented soya beans, sugar, garlic and chilli, it is commonly served with barbecued meats, especially fatty ones, and Peking duck. It also forms the base of many other Chinese-style sauces.

It is possible to buy ready-made hoisin, but here is my version, given to me by a Chinese chef friend.

makes 300ml

2 garlic cloves
1 red chilli, deseeded and finely chopped
100g black bean paste
4 teaspoons sesame oil
4 teaspoons rice wine vinegar or distilled white vinegar
75ml dark soy sauce
3 tablespoons molasses or honey

1 Put the garlic in a mortar and, using a pestle, crush it to a fine paste.

2 Add the chilli and crush again to a paste.

3 Add the black bean paste, sesame oil and vinegar, then stir in the soy sauce.

4 Heat the molasses or honey in a small pan and stir it into the paste. You may need to add more soy sauce or bean paste, depending on your preferred flavour balance.

ROAST DUCK PEKING STYLE

Traditionally, Peking-style duck takes an age to prepare: first the blanching of the ducks in boiling water to break down the fat, then drying the skins by hanging them in an airy place. The sight of some 50 ducks hanging on hooks around the perimeter of a Chinese kitchen is one of my favourite memories from my time in Asia. But don't panic – my adaptation of the dish here is far quicker and just as tasty.

serves 4

1 duck, about 1.7kg
4 tablespoons hoisin sauce (see left)
1 teaspoon peeled and grated fresh ginger
½ teaspoon Chinese five-spice powder
2 tablespoons runny honey
1 tablespoon light soy sauce
1 tablespoon sweet sherry
1 garlic clove, crushed

1 Blanch the whole duck in a large pan of boiling water (or hold the duck over the sink and very carefully pour boiling water over it, rotating it so that the skin is scalded). Dry well with a cloth.

2 Preheat the oven to 200°C/400°F/gas mark 6.

3 Put all the remaining ingredients in a pan and bring slowly to the bowl. Remove from the heat and brush liberally over the duck, inside and out.

4 Place the duck on a rack in a roasting tin and roast for 1½ hours, until caramelised and sticky, with a crisp skin. Turn the oven down to 180°C/350°F/gas mark 4 and cook for a further 40 minutes.

5 Remove the duck from the oven and leave to cool before cutting into pieces. Serve with sautéed shiitake mushrooms, steamed Chinese greens and some extra hoisin sauce mixed with a little hot water.

PG tip If you don't have a roasting rack, a cake cooling rack is fine.

ROAST DUCK PEKING STYLE

If you fancy striving for maximum authenticity, by all means try hanging the blanched and dried duck at room temperature for 5 hours before roasting – the skin should crisp up really nicely.

JAPANESE MUSTARD SAUCE

⊕ *Serve this hot sauce smeared on a thick, juicy steak or pork chop – it's just marvellous.*

makes 150ml

2 garlic cloves, crushed
1 tablespoon pickled ginger
1 teaspoon toasted sesame seeds
½ teaspoon wasabi paste (Japanese horseradish)
2 tablespoons Dijon mustard
1 teaspoon mirin (Japanese sweet rice wine)
1 teaspoon soy sauce

1 Put the garlic, ginger, sesame seeds and wasabi paste in a mortar and crush to a fine paste with a pestle.
2 Transfer to a bowl and stir in the mustard.
3 Add the mirin and soy sauce and mix well.

TERIYAKI

The name teriyaki derives from *teri*, meaning to give shine and lustre, and *yaki*, which refers to the grilling method of cooking. Traditionally the cooked ingredient is dipped in or brushed with sauce several times before and during cooking. The inclusion of molasses is not strictly traditional but I think it gives a really unctuous taste and shine. In Japan a little grated fresh ginger is also sometimes added.

You can buy teriyaki in bottles, but for me it just does not compare with the homemade variety, which is so easy to prepare. ⊕ *It goes wonderfully with fish, meat, poultry and vegetables – as a marinade, cooking sauce or glaze.*

makes 300ml

125ml shoyu (Japanese soy sauce)
2 tablespoons mirin (Japanese sweet rice wine)
1 tablespoon brown sugar
3 tablespoons black treacle or molasses

1 Put all the ingredients in a small pan and bring gently to the boil. Simmer for 10 minutes until syrupy, then leave to cool.

Variations

WASABI GINGER TERIYAKI

Add 1 teaspoon peeled and grated fresh ginger to the basic recipe and whisk ¼ teaspoon wasabi paste into the cooled, finished sauce.

BARBECUE TERIYAKI

Whisk 1 teaspoon Dijon mustard and the grated zest and juice of 1 small orange into the cooled, finished sauce.

BARBECUE TERIYAKI-GLAZED SCALLOPS (for 4 people)

Place 12 medium-large, cleaned fresh scallops, out of their shells, in a shallow dish, then pour over 150ml teriyaki sauce. Cover and leave to marinate for 1 hour in the fridge.

Cook quickly on a hot barbecue or grill pan for 1 minute on each side, brushing regularly with the marinade. At the same time heat another 100ml teriyaki sauce (don't use the marinade, as it has been in contact with raw fish). Serve the grilled scallops immediately, with some grilled baby leeks and the hot teriyaki.

CHIBA SAUCE

(wasabi mayonnaise)

Chiba sauce is a dipping sauce from Japan, ideal to serve with tempura, delicate herb leaves such as shiso (also known as perilla), vegetables, seafood or meat, or just as a spicy dip for French fries or crisps. If you are not familiar with wasabi, take care as it packs a punch – you might prefer to adjust the quantity according to your taste.

makes 200ml

½ teaspoon wasabi paste (Japanese horseradish)
150ml homemade mayonnaise (see page 30)
2 tablespoons whipping or double cream
2 teaspoons shoyu (Japanese soy sauce)

1 Mix all the ingredients together in a bowl. The sauce will keep in the fridge in a sealed container for 3–4 days.

SEAFOOD IN NORI TEMPURA BATTER WITH CHIBA SAUCE

serves 4

6 cleaned scallops, halved
12 large oysters, out of their shells
8 large tiger prawns, peeled
vegetable oil, for deep-frying
100ml chiba sauce (see left) and lime wedges, to serve

for the batter

20g plain flour
80g cornflour
1 sheet of nori seaweed, finely chopped
salt
175ml ice-cold water
1 large free-range egg white, lightly beaten

1 Make the batter by mixing the flour, cornflour and chopped seaweed in a bowl with a little salt.
2 Add the ice-cold water and beaten egg white and stir until just mixed: the batter should still be lumpy.
3 Heat the oil to 180°C/350°F in a deep-fryer or deep pan. Season the seafood and dip each piece into the batter, then drop into the hot oil. You will have to do this in two batches, so season and batter only half the seafood at this stage.
4 Deep-fry for 1 minute until golden and crispy. Remove with a slotted spoon on to kitchen paper and keep warm while you batter and cook the remaining seafood.
5 Divide the seafood equally between 4 serving plates and serve with the chiba sauce and lime wedges.

SWEET-AND-SOUR SAUCE

One of the most loved sauces in the Chinese repertoire. ⊕ *Serve it with crispy-fried pork or chicken, or as a dipping sauce – wonderful!*

makes 400ml

150ml rice wine vinegar
2 tablespoons sake or dry sherry
5 tablespoons soft brown sugar
2 tablespoons tomato ketchup (see page 167 for homemade)
2 teaspoons light soy sauce
4 teaspoons cornflour, mixed with 4 teaspoons water

1 Put the vinegar, sake or sherry, sugar, ketchup and soy sauce in a pan and bring to the boil. Reduce the heat and simmer for 4–5 minutes.

2 Stir the cornflour and water mixture into the simmering sauce and cook for a further 1 minute.

Variation

HUNAN SAUCE

This is best described as a spicy variation of sweet-and-sour sauce. Just add 2 tablespoons sweet chilli sauce or sambal oelek (see page 148) and a 2.5cm piece of fresh ginger, peeled and grated, to the basic recipe. A real treat cooked with chicken or prawns.

PG tip Sometimes diced fresh pineapple, sliced pepper, sliced spring onions or sliced carrots are added and cooked in the sauce before thickening.

CHINESE BLACK BEAN SAUCE

makes 300ml

2 tablespoons sesame oil
1 tablespoon groundnut oil
2 garlic cloves, crushed
2.5cm piece of fresh ginger, peeled and finely chopped
75g Chinese black beans, coarsely chopped
150ml well-flavoured chicken stock (see page 8)
3 tablespoons dark soy sauce
1 tablespoon mirin (Japanese sweet rice wine)
1 teaspoon sugar
1 teaspoon cornflour, mixed with 1 teaspoon water

1 Heat both oils in a wok over a high heat. Add the garlic, ginger and black beans and fry for 1 minute.

2 Add the stock, soy sauce, mirin and sugar, and bring to the boil.

3 Simmer for 2 minutes, then stir in the cornflour and water mixture until the sauce thickens.

STIR-FRIED BEEF WITH BLACK BEAN SAUCE (for 4 people)

Cut 750g beef fillet into thin strips. Heat a little groundnut oil in a wok or frying pan and add the beef in batches to ensure the wok or pan stays hot during the cooking. Cook for 1–2 minutes until sealed, then remove each batch to a plate and keep it warm while you cook the remaining beef. After the last batch, return all the beef to the wok with 200ml black bean sauce (see above) and cook for 2 minutes. Serve the beef in the sauce, with steamed broccoli and rice.

CLASSIC AMERICAN COCKTAIL SAUCE

This hot and zingy little cocktail sauce is a favourite throughout America. ⊕ *Serve it as a dip for shrimp and other seafood.*

makes 300ml

200ml tomato ketchup (see right for homemade)
2 tablespoons grated fresh horseradish
1 garlic clove, crushed
juice of 1 lemon
3 drops of Tabasco sauce
salt and freshly cracked black pepper

1 Mix all the ingredients in a bowl with salt and pepper to taste. The sauce will keep in the fridge for about 1 week, but will lose its freshness after a couple of days.

Variation

JAPANESE-STYLE COCKTAIL SAUCE

Grate a 5cm piece of peeled fresh ginger and add to the basic recipe, with 1 tablespoon shoyu (Japanese soy sauce).

CLASSIC AMERICAN KETCHUP

Ketchup first appeared in American cookbooks during the early 19th century, but as a general term for a sauce made of mushrooms, walnuts or fruits. Summer is the ideal time to make tomato ketchup, when the best, extremely ripe and well-flavoured tomatoes are available.

makes 1 litre

1kg very ripe, flavourful tomatoes, quartered
1 tablespoon tomato purée
300g onions, chopped
300g cooking apples, peeled, cored and chopped
1 litre distilled white vinegar or cider vinegar
20g mustard seeds
½ teaspoon dried chilli flakes
½ small stick of cinnamon
1 teaspoon ground mace
1 teaspoon black peppercorns
1 teaspoon sea salt
250g brown sugar

1 Put the tomatoes, tomato purée, onions and apples in a heavy-based preserving pan with half the vinegar, all the spices and the salt.
2 Bring the mixture to the boil, then simmer for 1¾–2 hours, stirring occasionally, until well reduced.
3 Strain the hot mixture through a coarse sieve into a clean preserving pan, discarding any solids.
4 Add the remaining vinegar and the sugar, then stir the mixture over a low heat until the sugar has dissolved.
5 Bring to the boil and simmer until thick and syrupy. Remove from the heat and leave to cool.
6 Once the ketchup is cold, pour it into clean, warmed, sterilised jars, if you are going to store it, and keep in a cool area. Alternatively, it will keep for up to a month in a covered container in the fridge.

SMOKY MUSTARD BARBECUE SAUCE

Make this a few days before you need it, to allow the flavours to develop. ⊕ *Use it to baste chicken pieces or pork spare ribs just before they have finished cooking – utterly delicious. My other tip is to spread it lavishly over a rare minute steak, slapped between crusty French bread.*

makes 300ml

2 tablespoons vegetable oil
1 onion, finely chopped
1 garlic clove, crushed
juice of 1 lemon
100g soft brown sugar or honey
4 tablespoons red wine vinegar
150ml tomato ketchup (see page 167 for homemade)
2 tablespoons Worcestershire sauce
1 tablespoon smoked paprika
75ml Mexican-style hot chilli sauce or ½ teaspoon Tabasco
1 teaspoon Dijon mustard
salt and freshly cracked black pepper

1 Heat the oil in a frying pan and add the onion and garlic. Cook for 5 minutes until soft and lightly browned.

2 Add the remaining ingredients, except the salt and pepper, and simmer for 8–10 minutes. Add salt and pepper to taste and serve.

BULGOGI SAUCE

(Korean barbecue sauce)

⊕ *This sesame-flavoured sauce, whose name literally translates as 'fire meat', can be used as a marinade as well as a sauce to serve alongside barbecued meat and poultry.*

makes 200ml

1 garlic clove, crushed
1 teaspoon toasted sesame seeds
½ teaspoon coarse salt
2 teaspoons sugar
2 tablespoons soy sauce
2 teaspoons toasted sesame oil
2 tablespoons water
2 tablespoons rice wine or dry sherry
3 spring onions, finely chopped
1 tablespoon hot chilli sauce or sambal oelek (see page 148)

1 Put the garlic, sesame seeds, salt and sugar in a mortar and crush to a fine paste with a pestle.

2 Add the remaining ingredients and mix well. The sauce will keep well for 2–3 days in a sealed container in the fridge.

CITRUS PONZU

(lime and ginger dressing)

Ponzu is a traditional dipping sauce or light dressing made from soy and citrus juice. It can be purchased ready-made from Japanese stores, but generally lacks the punch of any freshly made version. Yuzu is a Japanese citrus fruit, often difficult to obtain, but lime is the closest substitute. ⊕ *Fantastic as a marinade for scallops or fresh oysters.*

makes 150ml

2 tablespoons fresh yuzu or lime juice
2 teaspoons Japanese rice wine vinegar
1 tablespoon light soy sauce
2 teaspoons mirin (Japanese sweet rice wine)
1 tablespoon sake
1 teaspoon caster sugar
5cm piece of kombu (kelp seaweed)
2.5cm piece of fresh ginger, peeled and finely grated
½ teaspoon finely grated lime zest, blanched

1 Put all the ingredients, except for the lime zest, in a non-reactive bowl and stir until the sugar has completely dissolved.
2 Cover the bowl with clingfilm and refrigerate for 24 hours, to allow the flavours to meld.
3 To serve, remove the kombu and add the blanched lime zest.

JAPANESE SALAD DRESSINGS

You may not immediately think of Japan as a country of salad-lovers, but in fact in this modern world salad forms an integral part of everyday life there, especially among the younger generation. Here are three of the most common Japanese dressings. All are best served immediately, but they can be kept in the fridge for one day.

CREAMY SESAME DRESSING

⊕ *Especially good with salad greens, for a basic leaf salad.*

makes 150ml

2 tablespoons ground Japanese white sesame seeds (see tip on page 159)
1 teaspoon rice wine vinegar
2 tablespoons vegetable oil
1 teaspoon sugar
1 teaspoon soy sauce
2 tablespoons mayonnaise (see page 30)
1 shallot or small onion, finely chopped

1 Put all the ingredients in a bowl and whisk until amalgamated.

YUZU DRESSING

⊕ *Wonderfully fragrant and refreshing, and great with seafood.*

makes 150ml

4 tablespoons yuzu juice, fresh or bottled
1 tablespoon shoyu (Japanese soy sauce)
1 teaspoon sugar
6 tablespoons vegetable or groundnut oil

1 Mix all the ingredients in a bowl.

WASABI AND GINGER DRESSING

⊕ *Great with fish and shellfish, especially crab and oysters.*

makes 150ml

1 teaspoon shoyu (Japanese soy sauce)
2 tablespoons rice wine vinegar
1 tablespoon sugar
½ teaspoon sesame oil
4 tablespoons vegetable oil
½ teaspoon wasabi paste (Japanese horseradish)
2.5cm piece of fresh ginger, peeled and grated

1 Put the shoyu and vinegar in a bowl. Add the sugar and whisk well to mix.
2 Add the remaining ingredients and mix well.

CRAB, RADISH AND SEAWEED SALAD

Not only a wonderful salad, but extremely healthy and nutritious.

serves 4

120g wakame seaweed, soaked in warm water for 2 hours, then drained
50g hijiki seaweed, soaked in warm water for 10 minutes, then drained
6 red radishes, thinly sliced
75g mouli radish (Japanese white radish), peeled and thinly sliced
150g fresh white crabmeat
20g pickled pink ginger
150ml wasabi and ginger dressing (see above)
1 teaspoon toasted black sesame seeds, to serve

1 Put the drained seaweeds, radishes, mouli, crabmeat and ginger in a bowl.
2 Add the wasabi and ginger dressing, toss well and serve on individual plates, sprinkled with the sesame seeds.

SAFRAN Jaune
(p pot plein 70 Fr.)
25 gr 50 F
50 gr 90 F

EAST meets west

'Fusion' is a relatively new term, applied to a revolution that started in America in the late 1970s but has now been embraced in many parts of the world. Essentially it describes a style of cooking in which chefs experiment with techniques, ingredients and presentations from diverse culinary traditions, creating new, cross-cultural dishes. When it is done well, the results can be utterly inspired, but it has to be informed by a careful understanding of how flavours work together.

If you are bold enough to experiment with this culinary exchange, it is a very liberating way to cook. This chapter helps you discover the pleasures of adding chilli to a traditional French béarnaise sauce, Asian flavourings to an Italian pesto, and Japanese wasabi paste to a balsamic dressing. To some this might seem like heresy, but no one can deny that it opens up a world of exciting possibilities.

ASIAN VIERGE SAUCE

In this light, classic French sauce, traditionally based on olive oil, lemon juice, tomatoes and herbs, the spicy sambal, ginger and cumin add an exotic, lively kick. ⊕ *Wonderful with char-grilled chicken.*

makes 200ml

6 tablespoons olive oil
2 garlic cloves, crushed
½ teaspoon cumin seeds, lightly toasted
2.5cm piece of fresh ginger, peeled and finely grated
4 tomatoes, peeled, deseeded and chopped
1 teaspoon sambal oelek (see page 148)
2 tablespoons lemon juice
1 tablespoon chopped flat-leaf parsley
1 tablespoon chopped mint
salt and freshly cracked black pepper

1 Put the olive oil in a pan with the garlic, cumin seeds and ginger and heat gently for 1 minute over a low heat.
2 Add the tomatoes and cook for 3–4 minutes until they soften.
3 Add the sambal oelek, lemon juice, parsley and mint. Season to taste and serve.

CHILLI TARTARE

This is PG's take on a classic mayonnaise-based sauce, with a little heat added to the traditional version. ⊕ *Serve as you would for usual tartare, with fried fish and chips, or with seafood.*

makes 300ml

150ml mayonnaise (see page 30)
3 tablespoons chopped sweet dill-pickled cucumber
1 small red onion, finely chopped
2 spring onions, finely chopped
1 teaspoon superfine capers, rinsed and coarsely chopped
2 tablespoons chopped coriander leaves
½ teaspoon Tabasco sauce, or 1 green chilli, finely chopped
1 tablespoon sesame oil
salt and freshly cracked black pepper
grated zest and juice of ½ lemon

1 Put the mayonnaise in a non-reactive bowl. Add the remaining ingredients, except the lemon zest and juice, then cover and refrigerate for at least 1 hour.

2 Add the lemon zest and juice, and adjust the seasoning. The sauce will keep, in a sealed container, for up to 2 days in the fridge.

BALSAMIC WASABI DRESSING

I'm a great lover of Japanese eating, especially sushi, which I think I could quite happily live on! The balance of salty and hot Japanese ingredients is masterly. This Japanese-Italian alliance is basically a vinaigrette with Japanese overtones. ⊕ *Use it as you would a classic vinaigrette, to dress greens and salads, or as I like it, drizzled over a carpaccio of tuna, squid or octopus.*

makes 150ml

½ teaspoon wasabi paste (Japanese horseradish)
1 teaspoon tamari (Japanese soy sauce)
1 teaspoon sugar
1 tablespoon balsamic vinegar
1 tablespoon rice wine vinegar
1 teaspoon sesame oil
6 tablespoons olive oil

1 Put the wasabi and tamari in a bowl, then add the sugar and both vinegars and whisk well.

2 Whisk in the sesame oil, then the olive oil, and cover and chill until needed.

PG tip Tamari is a complex, dark and richly flavoured soy sauce made entirely from soya beans, with no wheat. Shoyu is a lighter Japanese soy sauce, made from half soya beans and half wheat. Tamari is especially good for the growing numbers of people adopting a wheat-free diet.

MY TUNA CARPACCIO

It goes without saying that you need the freshest possible tuna for this recipe.

serves 4

400g piece of tuna loin fillet
2 tablespoons extra virgin olive oil
75ml balsamic wasabi dressing (see page 179)
a little coarsely cracked black pepper
rocket leaves, sliced avocado and orange segments (optional), to serve

1 Wrap the piece of tuna in clingfilm and roll into a cylindrical shape, twisting the ends of the clingfilm to create a sausage effect. Transfer to the freezer for 2–3 hours or until firm but not completely frozen through.
2 Remove from the freezer and place on a chopping board. Cut across in very thin slices, using a long-bladed, very sharp knife.
3 Arrange the slices delicately over 4 individual serving plates, covering the complete area.
4 Brush the slices with a little olive oil, then drizzle over the wasabi balsamic dressing and sprinkle with a little cracked black pepper.
5 Decorate the middle of each plate with rocket, avocado and orange segments, if using. Serve with a little crisp, fresh bread.

Other quick-and-easy east-meets-west sauce derivatives

SOUTHWEST BEARNAISE

Add 2 deseeded, finely chopped red chillies to the finished béarnaise (see page 24). Great with grilled steak or grilled meaty white fish, such as monkfish.

CHINESE ROUILLE SAUCE

To add a little oriental charm to a seafood stew or fish soup, replace the chilli in the rouille recipe (see page 33) with 2 tablespoons hot chilli sauce (sambal oelek, see page 148) and add 1 teaspoon light soy sauce.

PICKLED GINGER AND TOMATO SALSA

For a Japanese-inspired salsa, dice some vine tomatoes, mixed peppers and garlic and put in a bowl. Add a little soy sauce, rice wine vinegar, sugar and a little hot chilli sauce (sambal oelek, see page 148) to balance the flavours. Finally, add some finely chopped pickled ginger and chopped coriander. Lovely added to a cold noodle salad or with cold seafood.

TAMARIND-MINT PESTO

Replace the basil in the basic pesto recipe (see page 77) with mint leaves and add a 2.5cm piece of fresh ginger, peeled and grated, and 1 teaspoon tamarind paste. Proceed as for the basic recipe. Lovely with grilled fish, grilled lamb or seafood.

THAI PESTO

Replace the basil in the basic pesto recipe (see page 77) with a 50/50 mixture of coriander and Thai basil leaves, then add 1 finely chopped red chilli and 2 tablespoons sesame oil. Fantastic for pouring over grilled mussels or other seafood such as grilled calamari, prawns or clams.

TOMATO MISO SAUCE

Follow the recipe for the classic French-style tomato sauce (see page 58), but after adding the tomato purée, add 2 tablespoons red miso paste, 1 tablespoon soy sauce and 1 tablespoon mirin (Japanese sweet rice wine). I love this with grilled salmon and stir-fried Asian greens.

THAI STEAK SAUCE

The beauty of this sauce is that it has a dual purpose: it doubles up as a basting sauce for steak, brushed on as it cooks, and an accompaniment for the finished dish. ⊕ *Enjoy it with steak or chicken; it will soon become a favourite.*

makes 150ml

2 tablespoons tamarind paste
4 tablespoons water
1 tablespoon nam pla (Thai fish sauce)
2 tablespoons palm sugar or soft brown sugar
2 garlic cloves, crushed
4 tablespoons tomato ketchup (see page 167 for homemade)
2 tablespoons sweet chilli sauce (see page 146)
1 tablespoon kecap manis (Indonesian soy sauce)

1 Put the tamarind paste and water in a pan and bring to the boil.

2 Add the remaining ingredients and cook for 2 minutes. Remove from the heat and leave to cool.

JAPANESE SALSA VERDE

Italian salsa verde is one of my favourite sauces. It has everything: piquancy, freshness and a touch of pungency. In this version, a little Japanese horseradish and peppery mizuna leaves add a Far-eastern touch to a classic sauce. ⊕ *I love it with salt-grilled mackerel fillets and sliced, hot new potatoes (see below).*

makes 200ml

1 teaspoon wasabi paste (Japanese horseradish)
150ml olive oil
25g flat-leaf parsley
15g mizuna or rocket leaves
4 tablespoons superfine capers, rinsed
1 tablespoon nam pla (Thai fish sauce)
2 garlic cloves, crushed
juice of 1 lemon

1 Put the wasabi paste in a bowl and slowly whisk in the olive oil.

2 Transfer to a blender, add the remaining ingredients and blitz to a coarse purée.

GRILLED MACKEREL WITH JAPANESE SALSA VERDE

(for 4 people)

Slash the skin of 8 cleaned and trimmed mackerel fillets and season liberally with coarse salt and a little pepper. Place on an oiled baking sheet under a very hot grill for 3–4 minutes on each side, until cooked. Slice 225g cooked new potatoes and, while they are still hot, mix with 1 thinly sliced red onion, 200g sliced small vine tomatoes and the juice of ½ lemon. Divide this mixture between 4 serving plates and top each with 2 cooked mackerel fillets. Drizzle with 100ml Japanese salsa verde and serve.

SPICY MANGO AIOLI

You can add all manner of ingredients to a basic aïoli, and this is just one version using Indian flavourings. ⊕ *It goes particularly well as a spread in a chicken sandwich or with smoked salmon and bacon – a tasty combination. Also great with grilled salmon or lamb chops.*

makes 150ml

2 teaspoons vegetable oil
¼ teaspoon asafoetida powder
¼ teaspoon black mustard seeds
4 curry leaves
2 tablespoons finely chopped mango chutney
1 small hot red chilli, finely chopped
salt
100ml aïoli (see page 33)

1 Heat the oil in a frying pan over a moderate heat and sprinkle in the asafoetida, mustard seeds and curry leaves. Fry briefly, until the seeds pop.
2 Add the chutney, chilli and a little salt, then cover and cook for 2 minutes to heat the mixture through. Remove from the heat and set aside to cool.
3 When the mixture is cold, add it to the aïoli; the sauce should be quite hot, creamy and pleasantly sweet.

THE ULTIMATE CHICKEN SANDWICH

A great sandwich – full of flavour and extremely filling!

serves 4

4 boneless, skinless chicken breasts, about 150g each
2 teaspoons tandoori spice paste
olive oil
8 rashers of streaky bacon
4 burger baps, halved
2 firm but ripe plum tomatoes, cut into thick slices
leaves of 1 crispy Romaine lettuce
4 slices of Emmenthal cheese
75ml spicy mango aïoli (see left)

1 Place the chicken breasts, one at a time, between 2 sheets of clingfilm and, using a kitchen mallet or rolling pin, pound to an even thickness of about 1.5cm. Brush the chicken breasts all over with the tandoori spice paste.
2 Heat a grill pan until very hot. Brush it with olive oil and add the chicken breasts. Cook for 2–3 minutes on each side or until cooked through.
3 At the same time, if there is room in the pan, cook the bacon until nice and crispy. Otherwise, remove the chicken and keep it warm while you cook the bacon.
4 Meanwhile, preheat the overhead grill to hot. Toast the baps until golden, then top the base part of each bap with sliced tomatoes, lettuce and cooked chicken breast.
5 Cover each chicken breast with 2 rashers of bacon and a slice of cheese, and place briefly under the hot grill to melt the cheese.
6 Top with a good dollop of spicy mango aïoli. Add the bap lid to each, and lightly press down.

YOGHURT CHILLI SAUCE

A wonderfully refreshing, cool sauce based on the idea of a zippy European cocktail sauce, encompassing many cultural twists and turns. ⊕ *Delicious for binding fresh crabmeat or prawns.*

makes 150ml

½ onion, finely grated
2.5cm piece of fresh ginger, peeled and grated
1 red jalapeño chilli, deseeded and finely chopped
¼ teaspoon ground turmeric
½ teaspoon sugar
75ml tomato ketchup (see page 167 for homemade)
1 teaspoon sambal oelek (see page 148), or to taste
3 tablespoons thick natural yoghurt
1 tablespoon chopped coriander leaves
salt and freshly cracked black pepper

1 Put the grated onion and ginger in a bowl, then stir in the remaining ingredients. Season to taste and serve.

MEXICO-VIA-MUMBAI SALSA

I came upon this Asian-style salsa quite by accident one day while preparing an Indian-themed dinner at home for friends. My wife had forgotten to pick up some yoghurt for a raita dressing for my starter. After raiding the fridge, I improvised with the ingredients I could find, and came up with this Indian-inspired salsa instead. It went down rather well, so I am happy to include it in this section of the book. ⊕ *Serve with Indian-style meats such as kebabs or tandoori chicken, or with grilled fish or seafood.*

makes 300ml

2.5cm piece of fresh ginger, peeled and finely grated
225g ripe but firm plum tomatoes, chopped into small pieces
75g cucumber, deseeded and chopped into small pieces
1 red onion, chopped
2 garlic cloves, crushed
2 tablespoons balsamic or rice wine vinegar
juice of 2 large limes
½ teaspoon ground cumin
2 tablespoons chopped coriander leaves
1 tablespoon chopped mint
1 tablespoon tamarind paste (see tip on page 187)
salt

1 Combine all the ingredients except the salt in a bowl, cover and leave at room temperature for 1 hour for the flavours to meld.
2 Add salt to taste before serving.

PG tip

MEXICO-VIA-MUMBAI SALSA

Tamarind paste, a traditional element of Asian cuisine, contributes a gently sour flavour with an undercurrent of tropical fruits. It can occasionally be found as fresh pods, but is more readily available in either compressed blocks or as a smooth purée-like paste in jars.

SOY KAFFIR BUTTER SAUCE

Kaffir lime is native to Southeast Asia, where cooks traditionally use the zest and leaves, generally in sauces, or simmered in soups and curries. Ordinary lime zest can be substituted if you can't find kaffir leaves. ⊕ *Any shellfish or grilled fish would be wonderful with this sweet, salty and sour butter sauce, made using French techniques.*

makes 200ml

50g unsalted butter, chilled
2 shallots, sliced
1.5cm piece of fresh ginger, peeled and sliced
50ml distilled white vinegar
100ml chicken stock (see page 8)
3 tablespoons kecap manis (Indonesian soy sauce)
100ml double cream
2 kaffir lime leaves
4 mint leaves
4 Thai sweet basil leaves

1 Heat 10g of the butter in a pan, add the shallots and ginger and cook for 2–3 minutes until lightly softened.
2 Add the vinegar and boil to reduce the liquid by half.
3 Add the stock, kecap manis and cream and bring to the boil.
4 Lower the heat and add the lime leaves, mint and basil leaves, then simmer for 5 minutes.
5 Remove from the heat, whisk in the remaining butter, then strain through a fine sieve before serving hot.

GRILLED LOBSTER WITH SOY KAFFIR BUTTER

serves 4

2 live lobsters, 750g each
a little salt and freshly cracked black pepper
25g unsalted butter, melted
1 tablespoon nam pla (Thai fish sauce)
soy kaffir butter sauce (see left)

1 Put the live lobsters on a small tray in the freezer for 2 hours. Remove the lobsters from the freezer and put straight into a large pan of boiling water. Return the water to the boil and cook for 4 minutes, then remove the lobsters from the water and cool. (This preparation can be done in advance.)
2 Preheat the grill for 10–15 minutes at its highest setting. Lay each lobster belly-side down on a chopping board. Cut in half lengthways, from head to tail, to give 4 halves in total.
3 Remove and discard the stomach sac and any intestinal tract that runs down the tail section alongside the shell.
4 Place the lobster halves meat-side up on a large baking tray. Season lightly, then brush liberally all over with the melted butter.
5 Place under the grill and cook for 6–8 minutes until cooked through.
6 While the lobster is grilling, put the nam pla and soy kaffir butter sauce in a pan and bring to the boil.
7 Transfer the cooked lobster halves to 4 individual plates, spoon over the sauce and serve.

PG tip It is not just the cost that can put people off cooking lobsters, but the killing of them too. This method with the freezer is the most humane way to do it: the lobsters simply fall asleep and die painlessly.

INDONESIAN GUACAMOLE

If you enjoy the famous Mexican guacamole, you'll love this easternised variation, overlaid with the delicate flavours of Indonesia. ⊕ *Use as a spread to go in smoked salmon or roast chicken sandwiches.*

makes 300ml

2 ripe (but not soft) Hass avocados
1 large vine tomato, cut into small dice
1 tablespoon sambal oelek (see page 148)
10 Thai sweet basil leaves, torn into small pieces
1 red onion, finely chopped
juice of 3 limes
salt and freshly cracked black pepper

1 Cut the avocados in half and remove the stones. Using a spoon, scoop out the flesh into a bowl, then mash with a fork.

2 Add the remaining ingredients, with salt and pepper to taste. If you are not serving immediately, return the stones to the bowl to prevent the guacamole from going brown.

CHINESE TAHINI SAUCE

I love this sesame-flavoured sauce and often serve it as part of a buffet salad, tossed with Chinese egg noodles. The tahini adds a richer flavour than using sesame oil alone. ⊕ *Toss noodles with the sauce at the last minute or use as a dipping sauce.*

makes 150ml

2 tablespoons rice wine vinegar
½ teaspoon sugar
50ml soy sauce
2 tablespoons sesame oil
¼ teaspoon dried red chilli flakes
1 tablespoon groundnut oil
1 tablespoon tahini (sesame seed paste)
2 garlic cloves, crushed
2.5cm piece of fresh ginger, peeled and finely chopped
4 spring onions, finely chopped

1 Heat the vinegar and sugar in a small pan until the sugar has dissolved, transfer to a bowl and whisk in the remaining ingredients. The sauce will keep in a sealed container in the fridge for several weeks.

LIME PICKLE VINAIGRETTE

There is something about lime pickle that I can't resist. I tend to eat most of it before the meal even begins, precariously piled on to spicy poppadoms, much to the annoyance of my fellow guests who never get a look in! ⊕ *Here is a play on an Indian-French vinaigrette idea; excellent served with grilled fish or grilled chicken, or poured over hot, steaming new potatoes.*

makes 150ml

1 tablespoon chopped lime pickle
1 tablespoon chopped mint
½ tablespoon chopped coriander leaves
4 tablespoons olive oil
juice of 2 limes
2 tablespoons classic vinaigrette (see page 62)
1 teaspoon nam pla (Thai fish sauce)
salt and freshly cracked black pepper

1 Put the lime pickle in a blender with the herbs and olive oil and blitz to a coarse purée.
2 Transfer to a bowl and add the remaining ingredients, with salt and pepper to taste.

ROCKET AND YUZU CHUTNEY

Here I add a twist to a traditional Asian-style mint chutney, but substituting rocket for some of the mint. If you can't find yuzu (see page 170), fresh limes will do. ⊕ *This chutney is great for drizzling over rice dishes.*

makes 150ml

a small handful of mint leaves
a small handful of rocket leaves
1 onion, chopped
juice of 2 yuzu (or limes), or 4 tablespoons bottled yuzu juice
2 tablespoons water
½ teaspoon garam masala

1 Put all the ingredients in a blender and blitz to a coarse purée, adding a little more water if necessary. Refrigerate in a sealed container for up to 2 days.

CAFFE` CONFETT
Bicerin
CIOCCOLATO Tobler in tazz
PASTIGLIE
Leone
CARAMELLE

SWEET sauces

A sweet sauce can transform the plainest dessert into a culinary masterpiece, whether it's hot chocolate sauce poured over a poached pear, a simple fruit coulis to accompany vanilla ice cream, or a sweet flavoured butter to melt over grilled figs or pancakes. A good range of dessert sauces will enrich your repertoire immeasurably, and they are not at all difficult or time-consuming to make. In this chapter you will find recipes for traditional favourites, such as a vanilla-laced crème anglaise or a richly indulgent toffee sauce, alongside lesser-known treasures, like Mexico's cajeta – a thick caramel sauce made with goat's milk. Simple flavoured syrups can be prepared for the store cupboard and used to add a special touch to many sweet dishes.

CRÈME ANGLAISE

Perhaps the greatest and best-loved of all dessert sauces. This is basically a creamy vanilla sauce, or custard, delicately flavoured with vanilla pods; it is also the basis for delicious vanilla ice cream.

makes 750ml

300ml full-fat milk
200ml double or whipping cream
1 vanilla pod, split lengthways
6 free-range egg yolks
120g caster sugar

1 Put the milk, cream and vanilla pod in a heavy-based pan. Bring to the boil, then immediately remove from the heat and set aside to infuse for 15 minutes.
2 Meanwhile, using a whisk, beat the egg yolks and sugar in a bowl until thick and creamy.
3 Pour the warm milk and cream mixture on to the egg mixture, whisking continuously.
4 Return the mixture to the saucepan and cook over a low heat, stirring constantly with a wooden spoon or spatula until the custard thickens and coats the back of a spoon.
5 Remove from the heat, strain through a fine sieve and either serve hot or leave to cool.

Variations

BRANDY SAUCE

Add 2 tablespoons brandy to the finished sauce. This also works well with calvados, rum or pear (poire) William eau-de-vie. Brandy sauce is traditionally served with Christmas pudding, but the variations are great with pies and fruit puddings.

ALMOND MILK ANGLAISE

Bring the milk and cream to the boil with 150g ground almonds, omitting the vanilla, and leave overnight to infuse. Strain and use the almond-infused milk and cream mixture as in the basic recipe.

CITRUS ANGLAISE

Replace the vanilla pod in the milk and cream infusion with 2 tablespoons grated and blanched zest of lemon or orange. You can also add 1–2 tablespoons lemon curd sauce (see page 214) to the finished custard.

HERB-INFUSED ANGLAISE

I love infusing custards with fresh herbs, such as mint, lemon verbena, lemon thyme...the list is only as limited as your imagination. Add to the milk and cream infusion instead of the vanilla, then strain before you pour it on to the eggs.

SPICE-INFUSED ANGLAISE

Replace the vanilla in the milk and cream infusion with 1 teaspoon either ground cloves or ground star anise, or a stick of cinnamon. Great with autumn fruits, such as pears and apples.

CHESTNUT ANGLAISE

Replace the sugar with 50ml chestnut honey, then stir 2 tablespoons chestnut purée into the finished sauce. A festive favourite of mine that usually makes an appearance around Christmas!

MOUSSELINE ANGLAISE

For a lighter custard, fold 100ml lightly whipped cream into the finished, cold sauce.

TEA OR COFFEE ANGLAISE

Replace the vanilla pod in the milk and cream infusion with 2 tablespoons good-quality loose-leaf tea, such as Earl Grey or jasmine. For a coffee sauce, add 3 tablespoons prepared espresso coffee or 2 tablespoons Camp coffee essence to the finished sauce.

PG tip Leaving the vanilla-infused milk overnight will allow the vanilla to permeate better, and will improve the flavour.

Crème anglaise variation

SAFFRON ANGLAISE

Replace the vanilla in the milk and cream infusion with a generous pinch of good-quality saffron, then proceed as for the basic recipe. I love this with chocolate tart or poached pears.

CRÈME PÂTISSIÈRE

This custard-style cream is one of the basics of the pastry kitchen, and is used in numerous desserts and as a filling for such delicacies as profiteroles, French pastries and tarts. Once made, it can be stored in the fridge, covered, for up to 2–3 days, but I find it is best to use it the same day. Even better than caster sugar here is vanilla sugar, if you have it.

makes 350ml

300ml full-fat milk
60g caster or vanilla sugar
1 vanilla pod, split lengthways
4 free-range egg yolks
2 teaspoons plain flour
20g chilled unsalted butter, cut into small pieces

1 Put the milk with half the sugar and the vanilla pod in a pan and bring to the boil. Remove from the heat immediately, then leave to infuse for 15 minutes.
2 In a bowl, whisk the egg yolks with the remaining sugar until thick and light. Whisk in the flour well.
3 Remove the vanilla pod from the milk and add the milk to the egg mixture, whisking constantly.
4 Return the mixture to the pan and bring it slowly to the boil over a low heat. Cook for 1–2 minutes, to allow the flour to cook.
5 Remove from the heat and whisk in the butter pieces. Leave to cool before using.

Variations

CHOCOLATE CRÈME PÂTISSIÈRE

Before you add the butter, stir 100g grated good-quality plain chocolate (60–70 per cent cocoa solids) into the warm sauce, until melted and smooth.

COFFEE CRÈME PÂTISSIÈRE

Add 2 tablespoons Camp coffee essence to the finished sauce before cooling.

ALMOND CRÈME PÂTISSIÈRE

Replace the milk in the basic recipe with almond milk.

ALCOHOL-INFUSED CRÈME PÂTISSIÈRE

Add 1 tablespoon of your preferred liquor to the finished sauce –for example rum, cointreau, kirsch or pear (poire) William eau-de-vie.

CHIBOUST SAUCE

Also known as crème Saint-Honoré, this is a lightened variation of crème pâtissière, used to fill profiteroles or to line the base of a fruit tart. Replace the flour with cornflour and fold in 2 beaten egg whites to the finished, cooled sauce.

PG tip One of the most common mistakes in making this cream is to undercook it. You absolutely must cook it for a minute or two after it has boiled; you will notice a dramatic change in consistency as it becomes shinier, smoother and thinner, rather than thick and pasty.

ZABAGLIONE

An Italian sauce, also often referred to by its French name, *sabayon*. Both are generally made with whipped eggs and Marsala wine, although other types of alcohol are often used instead of Marsala.

Many traditional zabaglione recipes do not include the whipped cream at the end, but I find it gives the sauce a better finish. ⊕ *It can be served warm, cold or frozen and is excellent with both fresh and poached fruit.*

makes 300ml

6 free-range egg yolks
65g caster sugar
60ml Marsala wine
100ml double or whipping cream, semi-whipped to soft peaks

1 Put the egg yolks, sugar and Marsala in a bowl. Set the bowl over a pan of simmering water, with the base of the bowl just above the water.
2 Whisk until the mixture becomes light and frothy, and doubled in volume.
3 Remove from the heat, then gradually add the semi-whipped cream, whisking all the time until amalgamated.
4 Serve immediately or pour into glasses and leave to go cold; either is delicious.

Variations

ORANGE SAUTERNES ZABAGLIONE

Add the grated and blanched zest of 1 orange to the egg yolks and replace the Marsala with sweet Sauternes. Wonderful with hot chocolate puddings.

HONEY ZABAGLIONE

Replace the sugar with 3 tablespoons honey and the Marsala with Vin Santo.

ORANGE AND BASIL ZABAGLIONE

Add the grated and blanched zest of 1 orange to the egg yolks and replace the Marsala with orange liqueur. Finish the zabaglione with 1 tablespoon finely chopped basil – wonderful with oven-baked oranges.

CHOCOLATE ANIS ZABAGLIONE

Replace the Marsala with Ricard or Pernod. Fold 50g melted white chocolate into the finished zabaglione. Superb with nectarines or chocolate mousse.

CHAMBORD ZABAGLIONE

Replace the Marsala with 4 tablespoons Chambord liqueur. My favourite way to serve this is to sprinkle some finely chopped candied stem ginger on a dish of raspberries, then pour over the Chambord sauce.

PG tip The Marsala can also be replaced by port, calvados or one of my particular favourites, Bailey's Irish Cream, which makes a wicked sauce to serve with warm pear tart.

CREAMED CARAMEL SAUCE

Making your own caramel sauce can seem rather a daunting task to many people, but it doesn't have to be that way! Make sure you have the pans and ingredients ready and to hand before you start, and follow the basic steps carefully. It takes practically no time at all and is delicious for all manner of desserts.

One note of caution: be extremely careful when cooking the sugar to caramel. Once heated, it will be considerably hotter than boiling water.

makes 450ml

50ml liquid glucose
200g caster sugar
300ml double cream
25g unsalted butter, cut into small pieces

1 Put the liquid glucose in a deep, heavy-based pan and warm it over a low heat, without letting it boil. (It is important to use a deep pan, as the mixture foams up.)

2 Add the sugar, increase the heat and simmer until caramelised to a rich, golden-amber colour, about 2–3 minutes; the more caramelised the sugar, the more intense the flavour.

3 Shake the pan to distribute the colour evenly, but do not stir. Use a wet pastry brush to brush any crystallising sugar from the sides of the pan.

4 Meanwhile, bring the cream to the boil in a separate pan, remove from the heat, then pour the warm cream into the hot caramel, taking care as it will splatter.

5 Add the butter pieces and whisk the sauce until smooth. Remove from the heat and leave to cool before serving.

Variations

SALT CARAMEL SAUCE

Replace the unsalted butter with 40g salted butter, plus an extra pinch of sea salt. Lovely served over ice cream or with a pear tart!

LIQUEUR CARAMEL SAUCE

Add 50ml of your favourite liqueur to the finished sauce.

VANILLA CARAMEL SAUCE

Add 1 split vanilla pod to the cream before bringing it to the boil, then proceed as for the basic recipe and strain before using.

ORANGE CARAMEL SAUCE

Add the finely grated zest of 1 orange to the sugar and caramelise as for the basic recipe. Leave to cool before adding 2 tablespoons orange-flavoured liqueur, such as Grand Marnier or Curaçao.

Clear caramel syrup variation

POMEGRANATE CARAMEL SYRUP

Bring the basic clear caramel syrup to the boil with 1 tablespoon pomegranate molasses. Allow to cool before adding 4 tablespoons grenadine syrup. Try it in the semifreddo recipe opposite.

CLEAR CARAMEL SYRUP

Whenever I make this clear syrup it reminds me of my time training in a pastry department. Back then, caramel was traditionally made in copper-based pans to retain a better overall heat. Now a heavy-based pan gives a good result.

makes 250ml

200g caster sugar
50ml liquid glucose
100ml hot water

1 Put the sugar, liquid glucose and 50ml cold water in a heavy-based pan and stir over a gentle heat with a wooden spoon until the sugar has dissolved.
2 Increase the heat and, as soon as the syrup reaches the boil, stop stirring and cook until dark caramel in colour.
3 Remove from the heat, leave to cool slightly, then thin with the hot water.

Variations

VANILLA CARAMEL SYRUP

Split a vanilla pod lengthways and scrape the seeds out into the pan of finished caramel. Add 60ml hot water, boil for 1 minute, then remove from the heat and leave to cool. Lovely with fruit tarts.

JASMINE CARAMEL SYRUP

Bring 100ml water to the boil, add 1 tablespoon jasmine tea leaves and remove from the heat. Leave to infuse for 1 minute, then strain, reserving just the liquid. Add the infused tea liquid to the finished caramel syrup, simmer for 2 minutes, then leave to cool.

COFFEE CARAMEL SYRUP

Add 1 tablespoon Camp coffee essence to the finished clear caramel syrup. Wonderful poured over poached pears or bananas.

ICED WALNUT SEMIFREDDO WITH POMEGRANATE SYRUP AND PISTACHIOS

serves 4

100g caster sugar
75g walnut halves
2 free-range eggs
75g white chocolate, melted
300ml double cream, semi-whipped to soft peaks
1 quantity pomegranate caramel syrup (see opposite)
2 tablespoons roughly chopped shelled pistachios

1 Put 60g of the sugar in a heavy-based pan over a low heat. Gently melt the sugar, then increase the heat until it cooks to a dark caramel-amber colour.
2 Add the walnuts and cook for 30 seconds. Pour the mixture out into a tray and leave to cool, then finely chop it into small pieces.
3 Put the eggs and remaining sugar in a bowl and set the bowl over a pan of simmering water. Whisk until the mixture doubles in volume and becomes thick, dense and creamy. Remove the bowl from the heat and whisk it again until cool.
4 Add the melted chocolate, then fold in the semi-whipped cream and the caramelised sugared nuts.
5 Pour into a clingfilm-lined terrine or individual moulds and place in the freezer overnight.
6 Remove the frozen semifreddo from the terrine or moulds. Cut the terrine into slices or, if using individual moulds, leave them whole. Pour over the pomegranate syrup, sprinkle with the pistachios and serve.

CAJETA SAUCE

I had to find a place in this book for this famous Mexican caramel sauce. It is traditionally made from fresh goat's or sheep's milk, cooked down very slowly until it becomes a luscious, enriched, caramelised cream. In Mexico it is sold in jars, but sadly I have found it hard to come by here, not for want of trying. Luckily, it's easy to recreate at home. ⊕ *Cajeta is traditionally served over ice cream or drizzled over pancakes, but I love it with roasted bananas, or even pumpkin pie served for Thanksgiving. I also spread it thickly over bread or brioche, a real treat. Make plenty – it doesn't stick around for long!*

makes 750ml

750ml goat's (or sheep's) milk
75g granulated sugar
250ml whipping cream
1 fat stick of cinnamon
50g chilled unsalted butter, cut into small pieces

1 Put the milk, sugar, cream and cinnamon stick in a wide, heavy-based pan and bring to the boil.
2 Remove the cinnamon, lower the heat and simmer gently for about 2 hours. It will go though varying colour changes in this time, from light to dark caramel.
3 Remove from the heat and whisk in the butter. Serve warm or leave to cool. The sauce will keep in a sealed jar in the fridge for 2 weeks.

VANILLA PANCAKES WITH ROASTED BANANAS AND CAJETA

serves 4

150g plain flour
1 tablespoon caster sugar
4 free-range eggs
1 vanilla pod or 1 teaspoon vanilla extract
150ml whipping cream
150ml full-fat milk
vegetable oil, for frying
25g unsalted butter
4 bananas, peeled and halved lengthways
2 tablespoons icing sugar
125ml cajeta sauce (see left)
natural yoghurt, to serve (optional)

1 Sift the flour into a bowl, stir in the caster sugar and eggs and mix well.
2 Split the vanilla pod lengthways and scrape out the seeds. Add the seeds, cream and milk to the bowl and mix well to form a smooth batter. Leave to rest for 1 hour.
3 Heat a little oil in a large, non-stick frying pan. Using a 5cm diameter ladle, spoon some of the batter in heaps around the pan, far enough apart to ensure they will not touch each other as they spread.
4 Cook until just golden round the edges – about 1 minute – then flip each pancake over and cook on the other side for a further 1 minute, until golden. Remove from the pan and keep warm. Repeat until all the batter is used up, making 8 pancakes in total.
5 Meanwhile, heat the butter in another frying pan and add the bananas. Dust with icing sugar and cook until golden and caramelised.
6 Place 2 banana halves between 2 pancakes on each serving plate. Pour over a little cajeta and top with a dollop of yoghurt, if using.

BUTTERSCOTCH SAUCE

The whisky is optional but traditional here. Adding golden syrup to the basic toffee sauce undoubtedly results in a more malty flavour.

makes 600ml

75g soft brown sugar
150ml double cream
50g unsalted butter
150g golden syrup
½ teaspoon vanilla extract
1 tablespoon Scotch whisky (optional)

1 Put the sugar, cream, butter and syrup in a heavy-based pan and cook gently over a low heat, stirring with a wooden spoon until the butter has melted and the sugar has dissolved.
2 Increase the heat and bring to the boil, stirring constantly. Lower the heat again and simmer for 8–10 minutes until the colour changes from a milky coffee to a rich caramel.
3 Remove from the heat, stir in the vanilla extract and whisky if using, and serve warm.

Variations

As with many sweet sauces, a dash of your favourite tipple (rum, brandy or Grand Marnier, for example) will always work. Or choose from the variations listed below.

CRÈME FRAÎCHE BUTTERSCOTCH SAUCE

Add 2 tablespoons crème fraîche to the finished sauce to add a little tanginess.

COCONUT BUTTERSCOTCH SAUCE

Replace half the cream with coconut cream and use 50g rather than 150g golden syrup.

GINGER BUTTERSCOTCH SAUCE

Add ½ teaspoon ground ginger to the ingredients at the start of the basic recipe.

TOFFEE SAUCE

This sauce and the butterscotch one on the left are often interchangeable, and indeed are basically one and the same. My research leads me to believe that toffee sauce originated in Britain and the Scots added golden syrup to create butterscotch sauce. Both are simple to make, rich and very moreish.
⊕ *Either sauce is wonderful poured over ice cream or served with steamed sponge puddings.*

makes 400ml

200g soft brown sugar
100ml double cream
100g unsalted butter
½ teaspoon vanilla extract

1 Make in the same way as butterscotch sauce (see left), but simmer for only 4–5 minutes so that the sauce does not turn as dark.

PG tip Both sauces can be prepared in advance and kept in an airtight container in the fridge for up to 10 days. Return either sauce to room temperature before serving.

CHOCOLATE SAUCE

If you start with good-quality chocolate, making a great-tasting chocolate sauce is a simple task. Different cooks prefer different chocolates but they all agree that it's vital to use one with at least 60–70 per cent cocoa solids. This is the one thing to get right; after that, some cooks use water, some milk, some cream. All work well in their own way, and create sauces of different qualities.

makes 400ml

250ml single or whipping cream
25g caster sugar
120g plain chocolate (60–70 per cent cocoa solids), broken into small pieces
25g unsalted butter

1 Put the cream and sugar in a heavy-based pan and bring slowly to the boil.
2 Immediately remove from the heat and, off the heat, stir in the chocolate and butter until melted and smooth.
3 Serve warm or leave to cool.

Variations

BOOZY CHOCOLATE SAUCE

Add 2 tablespoons rum, Grand Marnier or another preferred liquor to the finished sauce.

GINGER CHOCOLATE SAUCE

Infuse the cream and sugar with 1 teaspoon ground ginger, then proceed as for the basic recipe.

LAVENDER CHOCOLATE SAUCE

Infuse the cream and sugar with 1 teaspoon lavender leaves and proceed as for the basic recipe, but strain before cooling. This is also very good with the same quantity of rosemary or thyme leaves.

WHITE CHOCOLATE SAUCE

White chocolate, although not technically a chocolate at all, makes a good sauce alternative to the dark chocolate versions. My wife Anita is a bit of a white-chocolate-lover, so I often make this at home for her.

makes 350ml

200g white chocolate, grated or broken into small pieces
250ml double cream
4 tablespoons full-fat milk
10g unsalted butter
1 tablespoon kirsch (optional)

1 Melt the chocolate in a bowl set over a pan of simmering water.
2 Put the cream and milk in a separate pan and bring to the boil.
3 Pour the cream and milk mixture into the melted chocolate, then add the butter and stir with a wooden spoon until melted and smooth. Stir in the kirsch, if using, and serve warm or leave to cool before use.

Variation

Finish the chocolate sauce with 1 tablespoon aniseed liquor, such as Pernod or Ricard – delicious.

Fruit coulis variation

MANGO COULIS

Replace the red fruits with 2 ripe mangoes, peeled and cut into chunks.

FRUIT COULIS

Coulis, made from puréed, strained fruit, is one of the simplest of all the dessert sauces to prepare. Fruit sauces add not only a fresh taste to desserts, but also a splash of colour and fragrance. They are traditionally served cold, but can also be served hot.

Fresh or frozen fruits can be used for coulis, and how much sugar you add will depend on the variety of fruit used, as well as on its state of maturity; you will need to adjust the proportion of sugar to match these varying conditions. ⊕ *Wonderful served with fruit tarts, puddings, or simply poured over ice creams and sorbets – a winner every time.*

PG tip Take care not to over-blend the fruits, as I find it lightens the colour and removes their natural freshness. For fruits with a tarter flavour, such as redcurrants, add double the amount of sugar, bring to the boil and cool before blending.

RED BERRY COULIS

You can use just one type of berry for this sauce, or make up a mixture of soft summer fruits, as I have here.

makes 600ml

225g raspberries
225g strawberries, hulled
2 tablespoons icing sugar
1 tablespoon water
a few drops of lemon juice, to taste

1 Put the fruits in a blender with the icing sugar and water. Blitz for 20 seconds until smooth, then add the lemon juice.

2 Adjust the sweetness with more icing sugar if necessary, then strain through a sieve and serve.

Variation

NECTARINE AND PEACH COULIS

Replace the red fruits with 4 ripe nectarines or peaches. Remove the stones, cut the flesh into pieces and proceed as for the basic recipe.

BAKED LEMON PUDDING WITH RED BERRY COULIS

In this dessert the lemon juice provides not only the base for a wonderful light pudding but also a tangy lemon sauce, beneath it. The red berry coulis acts as the perfect balance for the tart lemon flavour.

serves 4

1 tablespoon plain flour
225g caster sugar
grated zest of ½ lemon, preferably unwaxed
4 tablespoons lemon juice
4 free-range eggs, separated
250ml full-fat milk
a pinch of salt
200ml red berry coulis (see page 211), **to serve**

1 Preheat the oven to 180°C/350°F/gas mark 4. Sift the flour into a bowl, then add the sugar and the lemon zest and juice.

2 In a separate bowl, beat the egg yolks and milk together. Add to the flour and sugar mixture and stir well to mix.

3 In a clean bowl, beat the egg whites with the salt until stiff, then, using a spatula, carefully fold into the pudding mixture.

4 Pour into 4 lightly greased, shallow, ovenproof dishes. Place in a baking tray and pour boiling water into the tray to reach half way up the dishes.

5 Bake for 45 minutes until golden, light and fluffy. Serve with the berry coulis on the side.

OTHER FRUIT SAUCES

The sauces that follow here are all standard recipes, and perfectly good for it. But that shouldn't stop you playing around with the basic recipes to add extra interest and complexity, by infusing them with flavours of your choice. Lemon verbena, for example, makes a wonderful addition to the lemon sauce.

JAM SAUCE

makes 250ml

150g good-quality jam (such as raspberry, strawberry, fig)
1 teaspoon arrowroot, mixed with 2 teaspoons water

1 Put the jam in a heavy-based pan with 75ml water and bring to the boil. Stir in the dissolved arrowroot, and cook for 1 minute.

2 Remove any scum from the surface of the sauce and strain through a fine sieve.

LEMON SAUCE

makes 350ml

grated zest and juice of 2 lemons
60g caster sugar
15g arrowroot, mixed with 2 tablespoons water

1 Put the lemon zest and juice in a heavy-based pan along with 300ml water and sugar and bring to the boil.

2 Whisk in the dissolved arrowroot and cook for 30 seconds, then strain through a fine sieve.

PG tip Other citrus fruits, such as grapefruit, mandarins, oranges and so on can be substituted for lemons, with the quantity of sugar used depending on the fruit.

LEMON CURD SAUCE

makes 250ml

225g caster sugar
120g unsalted butter
finely grated zest and juice of 3 large, unwaxed lemons
3 large free-range eggs, beaten

1 Put the sugar, butter and lemon zest and juice in a heavy-based pan.

2 Heat gently, stirring, until the sugar has dissolved and the butter has melted.

3 Add the eggs, stirring constantly over a low heat, until the curd thickens and leaves the sides of the pan clean. Remove from the heat and transfer to a jar. When cool, cover and refrigerate.

FLAVOURED SYRUP SAUCES

Sugar-based syrups are an easy way to prepare a simple yet delicious sauce for desserts. They are wonderful poured over ice cream, or drizzled over seasonal fruit salads or delicate mousses. I include two recipes, one for basic syrup and one for a caramel syrup: both form the base of many great sauces.

BASIC SYRUP

makes 250ml

100ml water
200g caster sugar
100ml liquid glucose

1 Put the water, sugar and liquid glucose in a heavy-based pan and stir with a wooden spoon until the sugar has dissolved.

2 Heat the syrup and as soon as it reaches the boil, stop stirring and cook for 1 minute, until a lightly thickened syrup sauce forms.

3 Remove from the heat, transfer to a bowl and leave to cool.

Variations

ORANGE BLOSSOM SYRUP

Put 1 quantity of basic syrup in a pan with the finely grated zest of 1 orange and the juice of 4 oranges. Boil for 2–3 minutes, leave to cool, then add 1 tablespoon orange blossom water.

GINGER AND LIME SYRUP

Put 1 quantity of basic syrup in a pan with 2 tablespoons stem ginger syrup, the juice of 3 limes and a finely diced, peeled 2.5cm piece of fresh ginger. Boil for 2–3 minutes, then leave to cool.

SOFT FRUIT SYRUP

Place a small colander over a bowl. Lay a muslin cloth inside the colander, then add 225g fresh or frozen soft fruit, such as raspberries, strawberries or blackcurrants. Bring 1 quantity of basic syrup to the boil in a small pan, then pour it over the fruits. Leave overnight in the fridge to let the fruits release their juices into the bowl, to give a clear syrup. Stir in 1 tablespoon of fruit liqueur such as kirsch.

LAVENDER SYRUP

Put 1 quantity of basic syrup and 1 teaspoon lavender leaves in a small pan and bring to the boil. Remove from the heat and leave to infuse for 30 minutes, then strain.

RED WINE SYRUP

Put 150ml red wine (Shiraz or Cabernet Sauvignon) in a pan with ½ stick of cinnamon, 1 clove and ½ vanilla pod and boil until reduced by half. Add 1 quantity of basic syrup and cook for 10 minutes, then strain and cool. Other wines such as Champagne, rum and port also make great syrup.

PG tip Always ensure the sugar has completely dissolved before bringing it to the boil, and remember not to stir once it has reached boiling point, however tempting that may be!

Basic syrup variation

HERB SYRUP

Blanch a good handful (50g) of the chopped herb of your choice – mint, basil and coriander are ideal – in boiling water for 10 seconds, then quickly remove to a bowl of iced water. Drain, dry, then blitz in a blender with the basic syrup. Strain through a fine sieve or piece of muslin.

MOROCCAN BAKLAVA WITH ORANGE BLOSSOM SYRUP

This is my version of the famous Greek dessert, popular throughout the whole Mediterranean region. The Moroccan element comes in the fragrance and light spicing synonymous with the country's cuisine.

serves 4

100g fresh dates, stones removed, finely chopped
175g walnut halves
175g whole almonds
60g granulated sugar
2 tablespoons orange blossom water
1 teaspoon ground cinnamon
¼ teaspoon ground cloves
100ml orange juice
18 sheets of filo pastry, 20 x 30cm
75g unsalted butter, melted
orange blossom syrup (see page 215), to taste

1 Put the dates, walnuts and almonds in a blender and blitz to a paste.

2 Transfer to a bowl, add the sugar, orange blossom water, cinnamon, cloves and 50ml of the orange juice and mix well. Preheat the oven to 160°C/325°F/gas mark 3.

3 Place a sheet of filo pastry in a 20 x 30cm baking tin and brush with the melted butter. Top with 6 more sheets of filo, brushing each sheet well with melted butter.

4 Spread half the nut filling evenly over the surface, then top with 6 more sheets of filo, brushing each sheet with butter.

5 Top with the remaining filling and the remaining filo sheets, brushing each sheet with butter in the same way.

6 Cut the baklava into diamond shapes in the tin and bake for 20–25 minutes, until an even golden colour all over. Remove from the oven and leave to stand for 5 minutes. Pour some orange blossom syrup over the top and serve.

SWEET COMPOUND BUTTERS

These sweet compound butters make a simple, very flexible sauce or topping for all manner of hot desserts, such as steamed puddings or crumbles. They are also delicious on warm toasted tea buns, pancakes, waffles, or simply toast. All the recipes below use 100g softened, unsalted butter and follow the method outlined in the savoury butter recipes on page 36.

LAVENDER HONEY BUTTER

Add 2 tablespoons lavender honey and ¼ teaspoon lavender leaves to the butter, then beat until smooth. Proceed as for the savoury butter, rolling it up in clingfilm. Especially good with figs.

RUM AND RAISIN BUTTER

Add 1–2 drops of vanilla extract, 2 tablespoons soft brown sugar, 60ml rum and 2 tablespoons soaked raisins to the butter, then beat until smooth. Proceed as for the savoury butter, rolling it up in clingfilm.

CINNAMON BUTTER

Add 3 tablespoons icing sugar and 1 tablespoon ground cinnamon to the butter, then beat until smooth. Proceed as for the savoury butter, rolling it up in clingfilm.

CHOCOLATE BUTTER

Add 125g finely grated, dark chocolate, 2 tablespoons icing sugar and 2 tablespoons crème de cacao liqueur to the butter, then beat until smooth. Proceed as for the savoury butter, rolling it up in clingfilm.

COFFEE BUTTER

Add 4 tablespoons icing sugar and 2 tablespoons Camp coffee essence to the butter and beat until smooth. Proceed as for the savoury butter, rolling it up in clingfilm.

GRILLED FIGS EN BRIOCHE WITH LAVENDER BUTTER AND GOAT'S CHEESE

I make these when I'm in the mood for something a little different for Sunday brunch.

serves 4

150g soft goat's cheese
1 tablespoon honey, melted
4 firm, ripe figs
100g caster sugar
4 slices of good-quality brioche
50g lavender honey butter (see left)

1 Preheat the grill to its highest setting. Put the goat's cheese and melted honey in a bowl and stir with a wooden spoon to mix and soften.
2 Cut the figs in half and sprinkle the cut sides with the sugar. Place under the hot grill until caramelised. (Alternatively, do this with a blow torch.)
3 Toast the brioche slices until golden and top each with 2 slices of lavender butter, then return to the grill to melt gently.
4 Place 2 fig halves on each brioche slice, with a good dollop of the goat's cheese on the side, and serve.

WEIGHT (solids)

15g	½oz
25g	1oz
40g	1½oz
50g	1¾oz
75g	2¾oz
100g	3½oz
125g	4½oz
150g	5½oz
175g	6oz
200g	7oz
225g	8oz (½lb)
250g	9oz
275g	9¾oz
300g	10½oz
325g	11½oz
350g	12oz (¾lb)
400g	14oz
425g	15oz
450g	1lb
500g	1lb 2oz
600g	1¼lb
700g	1lb 9oz
750g	1lb 10oz
1kg	2¼lb
1.2kg	2¾lb
1.5kg	3lb 5oz
2kg	4½lb
2.25kg	5lb
2.5kg	5½lb
3kg	6½lb

VOLUME (liquids)

5 ml	1 teaspoon
10ml	1 dessertspoon
15ml	1 tablespoon or ½fl oz
30ml	1fl oz
50ml	2fl oz
100ml	3½fl oz
125ml	4fl oz
150ml	5fl oz (¼ pint)
200ml	7fl oz
250ml (¼ litre)	9fl oz
300ml	10fl oz (½ pint)
350ml	12fl oz
400ml	14fl oz
425ml	15fl oz (¾ pint)
450ml	16fl oz
500ml (½ litre)	18fl oz
600ml	20fl oz (1 pint)
700ml	1¼ pints
750ml (¾ litre)	1½ pints
1 litre	1¾ pints
1.2 litres	2 pints
1.5 litres	2¾ pints
2 litres	3½ pints
2.5 litres	4½ pints

LENGTH

5mm	¼ in
1cm	½ in
5cm	2 in
7cm	3 in
10cm	4 in
15cm	6 in
18cm	7 in
20cm	8 in
24cm	10 in
28cm	11 in
30 cm	12 in

INDEX